THE PEOPLE OF NOWHERE

The Palestinian Vision of Home

DANNY RUBINSTEIN

Translated by Ina Friedman

TIMES BOOKS

RANDOM HOUSE

This work was originally published in Hebrew
as *The Fig Tree Embrace* by Keter Publishing
House, Ltd, Jerusalem, Israel, in 1990. Copyright
© Keter Publishing House, Ltd, Jerusalem.

A hardcover edition of this work was published by Times Books, a division
of Random House, Inc., New York, in 1991.

Library of Congress Cataloging-in-Publication Data

Rubinstein, Danny.
[Hibuk ha-te 'enah. English]
The people of nowhere: the Palestinian vision of home/Danny Rubinstein;
translated by Ina Friedman.
p.   cm.
Translation of: Hibuk ha-te 'enah.
ISBN 0-8129-2149-6
1. Palestinian Arabs—Attitudes.
2. Palestinian Arabs Government policy—Israel.
3. Jewish-Arab relations—1949–   4. Israel—Ethnic relations.   I. Title.
DS119.7.R75913   1991
305.892'75694—dc20   91-50186

Book design by Debbie Glasserman

Manufactured in the United States of America
2   4   6   8   9   7   5   3
First Paperback Edition

THE PEOPLE OF NOWHERE

FOREWORD

On May 15, 1948, the leadership of the Jewish community of Palestine, headed by David Ben-Gurion, formally proclaimed the establishment of the State of Israel as the sovereign country of the Jewish people. The creation of Israel was the realization of a dream that had been a central motif in Jewish life for close to two millennia. Since the loss of independence in the land of Israel and the destruction of the Second Temple in A.D. 70, Jewish civilization had been shaped around the longing to return from exile to the "land of Zion Jerusalem." But the longer that exile went on, the more abstract grew the Jews' yearnings for the land of their forefathers. Toward the end of the nineteenth century there was a turnabout: the rise of modern Jewish nationalism, in the form of the Zionist movement, encouraged and organized Jews to actually settle in Palestine. The aim of Zionism was more than to lay claim to a historic birthright and reinhabit an ancient homeland; it was to build a new, healthy Jewish society freed of the stifling conventions of Diaspora life. Zionism was not the prevailing ideology among the Jews of the day. Yet after decades of struggle, and especially after the Holocaust, which destroyed about a third of the Jewish people, the movement succeeded in establishing an independent Jewish state with a population of 650,000 Jews. Zionism had succeeded in coming to the forefront of world Jewish concerns.

That in itself was a stunning achievement, but it left many problems unresolved. Perhaps the greatest of these difficulties, then and now, was that the country to which the Jews laid claim was not, as they may have imagined, a land without a people awaiting their return. Palestine had in fact been inhabited for centuries by a variegated (though mostly Muslim) Arab population governed within the broad framework of the Ottoman Empire. Although this population was loosely tied to the surrounding Arab peoples, its homeland was Palestine. Its members served in the Ottoman institutions of government, and some were also active in the Arab national awakening at the start of the twentieth century.

The Arab nationalist movement, which gained strength and momentum following World War I, was not monolithic. It focused on the individual sectors of the Arab world that had been divided among the European imperialist powers; and separate struggles for independence were mounted in Egypt, Syria, Lebanon, Iraq, North Africa, and Palestine, which came under a British Mandate in 1920. However, the situation in Palestine was unique: the British administration was obliged to make good on the pledge made in 1917 by

Foreign Secretary Lord Balfour to create a "national home" for the Jews there, while during the war promises had also been made to grant independence to Arab states throughout the region. For the next several decades, it remained unclear how the British government could possibly fulfill its undertaking to turn the same country into both an independent Jewish and an independent Arab state.

From the outset of the British Mandate, violent clashes erupted periodically between the rival Arab and Jewish camps and spiraled to a height in 1936 with the Arab Revolt against both the British and the Jews. Successive royal commissions tried to hammer out a compromise solution to the competing claims on Palestine, but all of them failed, and in 1947 an exasperated British government dropped the problem in the lap of the newly created United Nations. The UN created a commission of its own to study the conflict and decided that, rather than honor the national rights of one community at the expense of the other, the answer lay in simple division: in November 1947 the General Assembly passed a resolution calling for the partition of Palestine into two states, Jewish and Arab. Strictly speaking, the UN had no formal jurisdiction over the area and could not force the sides to accept its ruling. In any event, the Jews of Palestine agreed to partition (though not without misgivings); the Arabs categorically rejected it. And it was against this background that violence again broke out at the end of 1947. By the following spring it had developed into a full-scale war between the newly established State of Israel and the surrounding Arab countries, which came to the aid of Palestine's Arabs.

It was this war that created the Palestinian refugee problem, as masses of people fled or were driven from their homes in the course of the fighting. To cope with the immediate plight of these homeless people, the United Nations set up refugee camps in those parts of Palestine which had been under the British Mandate that remained in Arab hands, namely, the West Bank and Gaza Strip. Similar facilities were created under its auspices for those Palestinians who had fled to neighboring Arab states—in particular, Lebanon and Syria. These camps were meant to be temporary; however, they became more permanent as the refugee problem lingered and festered for close to a generation.

Then matters took a somewhat ironic turn. In May 1967 Egyptian President Gamal Abdul Nasser, in a decidedly feisty mood, set off a chain of events that quickly culminated in the brief and punishing Six-Day War. Within hours Israel found itself in control of both the West Bank and Gaza Strip, and consequently of more than half of the total Palestinian population. The Israelis immediately established a military government in these occupied territories, and it was in the shadow of their rule that the Palestinian national movement— which had been a marginal force until the mid-1960s— steadily grew and flourished. At first, the new Palestinian leadership—the PLO—conducted a modest but irksome armed struggle against Israel from the neighboring Arab states of Jordan (until 1971) and then Lebanon (from 1972 to 1982), where the Palestinians took advantage of the long civil war to build something of a state within a state. After Israel's 1982 invasion of Lebanon and siege of Beirut, the PLO leadership was forced into ignominious exile far from the arena of struggle, taking up new headquarters in Tunis.

But this setback did not spell the end of the Palestinian national struggle (as various Israeli leaders had claimed it would). Even after Egypt had withdrawn from the circle of violence by signing a separate peace treaty with Israel in 1978, the Palestinians continued to press their national claims and oppose Israeli rule in an effort that reached its peak in the late 1980s in the popular uprising known as the *intifada*. Though it began as a spontaneous outburst of pent-up anger and frustration, the *intifada* was soon molded into a struggle of a new kind with a dual purpose: not only to drive the Israelis out of the occupied territories by making their occupation untenable, but also to shake the Palestinians out of their passivity and instill the belief that they need not wait for salvation from afar. They could no longer rely upon guerrillas stealing over the border or sovereign governments championing their cause. This new outlook maintained that the Palestinians must look only to themselves.

Despite its initial success in galvanizing world public opinion, the *intifada* gradually retreated into the background and became almost routine. More to the point, despite three years of defiance and struggle, it failed to modify the thinking of Israel's Likud-led government, which advocates permanent Israeli rule and accelerated Jewish settlement in the occupied territories. By the summer of 1990, disappointment in the uprising's achievements and bitterness over the world's indifference to their plight had driven the Palestinians and their leadership abroad to again seek salvation from outside sources—this time in the figure of Iraqi strongman Saddam Hussein after his unprovoked invasion of Kuwait. With the onset of the Gulf crisis, the Palestinians chose to believe that the world would accept a "linkage," at least in principle, between an Iraqi withdrawal from Kuwait and an Israeli withdrawal from the territories occupied since 1967. The dire outcome of the Gulf War only heightened their despair. Not only had their support for Saddam proved futile, it turned the oil-rich countries of the Gulf region against them, depriving the PLO of the steady flow of funds it had enjoyed from the Gulf. As a result, toward the middle of 1991 the Palestinians again turned their gaze inward and set to reassessing the course of their struggle against Israel.

Both sides in this ongoing struggle, Arabs and Jews, inhabit the same country. The two communities live alongside each other, yet the cultural and psychological distance between them is immense. Each one's perception of the other is based as much on prejudice, fear, and suspicion as on direct personal experience. The conceptual world of the Palestinian refugees, most of whom live in camps to this very day, is even more difficult for outsiders to penetrate.

CONTENTS

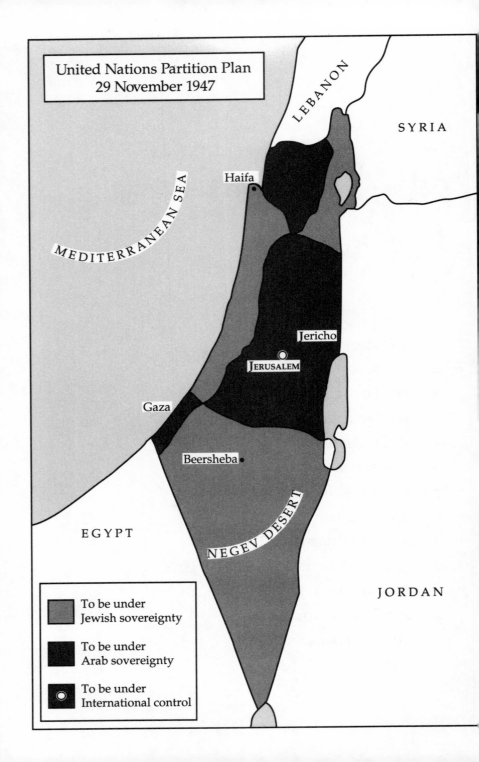

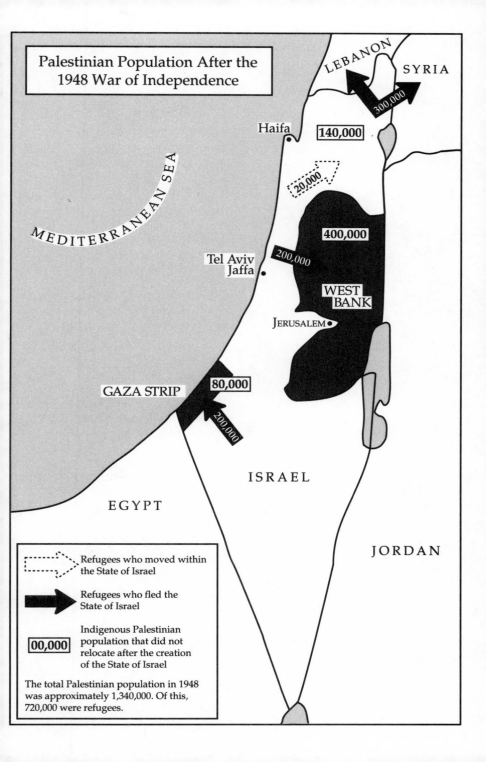

THE PEOPLE OF NOWHERE

1

VICTIMS OF
THE MAP

In Israel's 1948 War of Independence over 700,000 Arabs, half of the Palestinian population, were uprooted from their homes and their land. After the fighting had ended, the United Nations agencies reported the existence of some 720,000 refugees, whereas Israeli sources spoke of 550,000 and the Arabs claimed the number was more than 900,000. During the war the Arabs of Palestine lost hundreds of villages, towns, and cities within the territory that became the Jewish state. The circumstances under which they became homeless were, and continue to be, a matter of controversy. Having rejected the UN Partition Plan of November 29, 1947, the political leadership of the Palestinian-Arab community embarked upon a war against the country's Jewish community. It was fought first by local forces (aided by volunteers from the neighboring Arab states) and then by the regular armies that invaded the country upon the establishment of the State of Israel (May 15, 1948) with the aim of destroying it.

Various kinds of military units engaged in that long and costly war, particularly on the Arab side, and the fighting differed from place to place and time to time. So did the circumstances in which the Palestinians were displaced. Many of them fled when the war closed in on their homes or their villages became battlefields. In a number of places Israeli troops drove the Arabs out, especially after the invasion by regular forces from the Arab states, because they feared having to take on the invaders while a large Arab population was at their backs.[1]

When the war ended in 1949 and Israel signed armistice agreements with Egypt, Jordan, Syria, and Lebanon, the Arabs of Palestine were divided among five different sovereignties: the minority, some 160,000, remained within Israel and were granted citizenship, though they were subject to a military government for the next seventeen years; 200,000 went to Judea, Samaria, and East Jerusalem—later known as the West Bank—joining the local Palestinian population as citizens of the Hashemite kingdom of Jordan; some 200,000 others reached the Gaza Strip, turning the area's indigenous population into a minority. Both these classes of the population remained devoid of citizenship when the strip came under Egyptian military rule, and Gaza effectively turned into one huge refugee camp. Some 300,000 other refugees who made their way into Lebanon and Syria were likewise denied citizenship in these countries. Most of them concentrated along the Lebanese coastal strip and around Beirut, with a few settling in the area of Damascus.

At the beginning of the 1990s, over forty years after the upheaval in Palestine, the burgeoning number of displaced Palestinians is still being counted and still in dispute. We are no longer speaking of the first generation of refugees, who personally experienced the march into exile, but mostly of their children and grandchildren. According to the estimate of the United Nations Relief and Works Agency (UNRWA), which tends to the needs of these refugees, they now number in the area of two million people. Less than half of them (about 800,000) are still living in refugee camps in the West Bank, Gaza Strip, Jordan, Lebanon, and Syria.[2]

A refugee, of whatever generation, can be defined according to official formulas.[3] But far more important in terms of political realities is a man's subjective view of his status and whether the members of his community accept him or treat him as an outsider. Hardly any thorough and reliable research has been done to determine the status of the Palestinian refugees and map their dispersion. The fact that about one third of the Palestinians live in refugee camps or slums on the fringe of cities in the West Bank, Gaza Strip, and the Arab states to the north and east of Israel is enough to indicate that the problem of the 1948 refugees still festers decades after the fact and remains the prime obstacle to a political settlement in the Middle East.

The popular uprising *(intifada)* that broke out in the West Bank and Gaza Strip at the end of 1987 involved all the residents of the occupied territories but found its most vigorous expression in the refugee camps. In the painful chronicle of the Arab-Israeli dispute, December 9, 1987, has been fixed as the official anniversary of the *intifada*. It was on that day that riots broke out in the Jebalya refugee camp north of Gaza (the largest in the territories) and spread to the Balata camp just outside of Nablus (the largest on the West Bank). These cramped and squalid collections of houses and hovels are the heart of what is referred to as the "Palestinian problem," which is the core of the Arab-Israeli conflict. That fact was well expressed by a young man from the Deheishe refugee camp, south of Bethlehem, who pointed at a group of Israeli soldiers at the start of the *intifada* and told a television reporter: "They defeated all the Arab armies in six days [in 1967], but in over twenty years they haven't managed to conquer Deheishe!"

The chances of reaching a political settlement in the Middle East depend not only on solving the predicament of the Palestinian refugees but also on complex political developments in the Arab countries, Israel, and the world at large. This essay does not aspire to enter into all the aspects of the conflict. It is limited to various facets—including the political implications—of the sense of homelessness that has enveloped most of the Palestinians since 1948. "Exiles from history and homeland" is what the poet Mahmoud Darwish has called his people;[4] they have been turned into "victims of the map."[5] They are "the people of nowhere," or as Edward Said has put it, the people who live "in a utopia, a *nonplace*, of some sort."[6]

For years the tragedy of the Palestinian refugees placed their demand to return to their land and homes at the top of the Arab agenda. The "right of return" draws its authority from a number of United Nations resolutions, primarily the one passed by the General Assembly on December 11, 1948, stating that: "The refugees wishing to return to their homes and live at peace with their neighbours should be permitted to do so at the earliest practical date." The demand to honor that right has been raised for over forty years in every political debate on the prospects of forging a settlement between Israel and its Arab—particularly Palestinian—neighbors.

Yet the unequivocal opposition to the return of the Palestinian refugees to lands within the Jewish state is shared by all the parties across the political spectrum in Israel. As far back as the final months of 1948, Jewish refugees flowing into the new state from displaced persons' camps in Europe and detention camps on Cyprus took over many of the homes and much of the land of the absent Palestinians. The Israel Defense Forces (IDF) and other arms of the Israeli government destroyed some of this property during the war,[7] so that from the outset it was almost impossible for Israel to agree to the return of refugees according to the terms of the UN resolution. The United States placed pressure on Jerusalem to take 250,000 refugees back as a gesture, and during the Lausanne Conference in the spring of 1949 the Israeli government decided to allow 100,000 refugees to return. But the Arabs rejected the offer out of hand.

To relinquish their right of return is utterly unthinkable to the Palestinians. "Usually a man lives in a certain place in the world, but for the Palestinian the place lives in the man," wrote the literary critic Anton Shalhat in 1987.[8] That sentiment sums up the Palestinian's political position on the issue of return and bespeaks a profound feeling that unites the Palestinian public as a whole. Clearly, however, what divides Israelis and Palestinians is not confined to the refugee problem—a point that comes out especially in the Palestinian attempts to change the clause in UN Security Council Resolution 242 defining them as refugees. These efforts have been going on for years. The PLO understands only too well that allowing the Palestinians to be stamped as refugees will earn them humanitarian aid but not recognition as a nation entitled to a state of its own.

This essay of the right of return and the Palestinian attitude toward it since 1948 is based primarily on literary works and other documents written by Palestinians themselves. These include novels and short stories, the poetry of longing, plays, films, sketches, journalistic pieces, memoirs, academic studies, and the minutes of political discussions. Naturally as an Israeli, I make no claim to detachment or even to the ability to divorce myself from my own hopes and fears regarding these issues. Neither can I avoid drawing comparisons between the Palestinians' attachment to their land and my own feelings toward it. But this book is not about such comparisons. Rather, its intent is to clarify the issue of the refugees and their right of return.

In every war or violent conflict of this kind, there is a tendency for both sides to depict the enemy as a monstrous, satanic figure in a bid—conscious or otherwise —to "dehumanize the enemy." Exploring the unremitting problem of the 1948 refugees is an attempt to grapple with this impulse while highlighting the human suffering that has turned the Israeli-Palestinian conflict into such a tense and implacable one.

2

THE HOUSE OVER
THE BORDER

The number of Arab settlements destroyed within the State of Israel in 1948, according to Dr. Sharif Kana'ne of Bir-Zeit University, who has been documenting these statistics for years, is 450.[1] One of them, Sataf,[2] is a ruined and abandoned village in the part of the Judean Mountains known as the Jerusalem Corridor.[3] A narrow mountain road leads to the village from Ein Karem, now part of western Jerusalem, and from the peak above it one can see the tortuous course of the Sorek River (Wadi Sarar) and the corridor settlements leading down to the coastal plain.

The village that used to be Sataf was a relatively small one. In 1941 it had 448 residents, all of them Muslims, living in a few dozen stone houses spread over just five and a half acres. They made their living from fruit orchards, field crops worked on just over 1,000 acres of terraced slopes and shallow wadis. Sataf, along with hundreds of other cities, villages, and even permanent

Bedouin encampments, is the subject of *Our Country Palestine*, by Mustafa Murad Dabbagh, a kind of Palestinian Baedeker. Dabagh began writing this eleven-volume history in Jaffa in about 1948 but did not start publishing it until 1966 in Beirut (Dar al-Taliyah Press). Since then this popular series has gone through many printings, although it is essentially a survey of places that no longer exist, a "guide to nowhere." Indeed, at the close of the description of Sataf, as in the descriptions of many other places, we read: ". . . and in 1948 the village was destroyed, with its inhabitants scattered everywhere."

In the autumn of 1949, after the establishment of the State of Israel, a village for new immigrants called Bikurah was founded at the top of the mountain. It was abandoned shortly thereafter, however, and Sataf became a military base and training ground for the elite commando unit 101 led by Ariel Sharon. Here too, as in places throughout the State of Israel, the Arabic name for the place was changed to a Hebrew one. "Drawing a map and determining names are an act of taking possession, of creating a new reality," writes Dr. Meron Benvenisti,[4] and so the Arabic Mount Sataf became the Hebrew Mount Eitan, and its bubbling spring was called the Bekorah Spring.

Refugees and émigrés the world over—and particularly in the United States and Australia—have brought to their new homes the names of the places they left. This has rarely happened in Palestine. But when it has happened the inhabitants have not really moved away. The inhabitants of Walaja, for example—also located west of Jerusalem—rebuilt their homes on the ridge facing their destroyed village and called it Walaja as well.

Dozens, perhaps even hundreds of names like Lydda, Haifa, Jaffa, and Ramle have been bestowed upon schools, streets, squares, whole neighborhoods, and even businesses wherever the refugees of 1948 live. But these names have never been given to new settlements. Those names remained firmly attached to places that no longer exist.

Anyone who happens to find himself at an early-morning hour near the exit from the Jebalya refugee camp in Gaza, or other places where Palestinian laborers assemble to travel to work in Israel, can hear the names of these vanished cities and villages. In announcing their destinations, the drivers who transport these workers refer to a lost map, calling out names like Faluja (rather than Kiryat Gat), Qastina (rather than Kiryat Malachi), Isdud, Yazur, Zarnuqa, and other places that disappeared from the map over forty years ago. An interesting instance of conferring a name as an act of taking possession is related to the town of Yehud (from the same root as Judah and Jew) near Ben-Gurion Airport. The traditional Arab name of the settlement was Yehudia, which may have been derived from the biblical Yehud in the territory of the Tribe of Dan. The town was settled during the first half of the nineteenth century by Arabs who had migrated from Egypt, and it continued to be called Yehudia until the struggle between the Arabs and Jews of Palestine reached crisis proportions. By then the Jewish associations of the name Yehudia made the inhabitants of the village uneasy, for these suggested the presence of Jews there in the past, and by extension, it suggested Jewish ownership. Gradually the Arabs not only of Yehudia but of Palestine as a whole began calling the town Abassiya, after the neighborhood in Cairo where most of the founding settlers originated. Since 1948 the Palestinians have used only the name Abassiya in all their references to the place, while in Israeli sources the name of the deserted Arab village has always been only Yehudia.

Over the years pine trees have been planted around Sataf on Mount Eitan and by the Bekorah Spring. Some of the village's houses and part of its ancient water system were restored, turning Sataf into a "model of mountain agriculture" and one of the more popular sites for outings and nature walks in the Jerusalem area.

One summer day in 1988, when the site was filled with Israeli visitors, shouts were suddenly heard from an elderly woman in traditional Palestinian village dress. She was ranting against the Israelis at the top of her lungs, in the rural dialect of Arabic characteristic of the area. It turned out that the woman was a native of Sataf who now lived in a refugee camp near the West Bank city of Ramallah. One of her sons, who was living in Kuwait, had brought his family for a visit, and she took them all to her native village—a custom widespread among refugees. The woman's ire had been kindled by an error in the restoration. She discovered, to her outrage, that the wall rebuilt next to the well should not have reached as far as the mulberry tree. "It's a lie," the old woman shouted. She recalled that her little sister had once fallen there, so there couldn't have been a wall. "How could they do such a horrible thing?" she wailed in deep-felt indignation. Her son, formally dressed in a suit and tie, seemed embarrassed by his mother's outburst. By the looks of him, he had been an infant when the family left Sataf and may even have been born in the refugee camp. Yet he also understood his mother's exasperation. It was as if she were saying: Isn't it enough you Israelis have stolen Sataf from us and taken it for yourselves? Now you're also falsifying, distorting, trying to steal my past as well, to obscure my history and the history of my village. As far as she was concerned, "stealing the past" added an additional sin to the original crime. Her teenage grandchildren looked somewhat alarmed as they guided her away from the milling Israelis, who didn't understand what the commotion was about: it was only a restored wall deviating slightly from its original course. But the old woman's reaction bore a message that the Israelis had completely missed. For the first generation of Palestinian refugees, the meaning of "homeland" was very simple, concrete, direct: a field, an olive tree, a veranda, a well. Hence their loss was felt immediately, and deeply, as a great tragedy.

Aref al-Aref, one of the most prominent Palestinian Arabs during the British Mandate (1920–1948), was among the first to call the 1948 defeat a "catastrophe" (*nakbah,* in Arabic). He entitled the five volumes documenting the destruction of his homeland *The Holocaust, the Destruction of Jerusalem, and The Lost Paradise,*[5] an apt expression of his people's deep despair in the period immediately after the war. "The Palestinian does not construct his life outside Palestine," wrote Edward Said. "He cannot free himself from the scandal of his total exile."[6] Hundreds of Palestinian intellectuals, writers, poets, and public figures have written of this tragedy, of the "lost paradise" whose inhabitants "were scattered everywhere" and became "the people of nowhere." But if we take a close look at the facts, this is something of an exaggeration—since only half of the

Palestinians were uprooted. The overwhelming majority of the Arabs living in Palestine in 1948 remained in
their homeland. Some 600,000 of them never left their
homes, while over 400,000 others became homeless but
remained within the bounds of what had been Palestine
under the British Mandate. According to estimates dat-
ing to the early 1950s, over 200,000 refugees moved to
the West Bank, which was annexed to Jordan, and
about the same number were crowded into the Gaza
Strip. Only some 320,000 of the original Palestinian-
Arab population moved beyond the country's borders.
And they did not move very far—not overseas or beyond the desert, but right next door to the East Bank of
the Jordan, Lebanon, and Syria. Why, then, has their
exile been portrayed in such dire terms?

Obviously some of the descriptions of the Palestinian
catastrophe and exile were designed to serve political
ends. Israeli spokesmen have often argued that the Palestinian leadership and the Arab states have cultivated
the myth of the "loss of the homeland" with cruel cynicism, so that it would serve as a weapon in their military and political campaign against the State of Israel.
Yet there is no question that behind the ostensibly calculated, political dimension of the issue lies a grain of
truth: a genuine sense of displacement that gripped the
refugees and spread a feeling of disaster throughout the
Palestinian community. Even if the Arabs have ex-
ploited the suffering of the refugees for purely political
ends, the architects of Palestinian policy and culture
based themselves on a reality when they described the
great distress of the exiled population.

In Palestinian-Arab society, as in other traditional societies, the tie with the native village was the strongest

of all. Palestinian nationalism, which began to emerge in the first half of this century, never really forged the hallmarks of a modern nation before the disaster of 1948. In fact, more than it instigated the struggle against Zionism, it was the struggle against Zionism that created the Palestinian national movement. Ties of tribal tradition bound the identity of all the Arabs of Palestine to specific villages, neighborhoods, and houses. These ties were typical of a mostly rural, agrarian society whose memories of the transition to sedentary life were still fresh. It was as if the Bedouin that were still in the vicinity were "breathing down their neck." In such societies the curse "May your house be destroyed" is still the worst imprecation of all. As soon as the woman from Sataf was removed from her house in the village, even by just a few kilometers, she was in exile. Those forced to relocate just a little way from their homes felt uprooted. In some cases the move was from one neighborhood in Jerusalem to another or from one side of the street to another—and that was enough to make them feel displaced.[7] These refugees remained in their country, continued to speak their own language, and lived among their people and co-religionists but nonetheless regarded themselves as rootless and deprived of a homeland.

Among the Arabs who remained within Israel and became citizens of the new state were some refugees. The most renowned were the inhabitants of Biram and Ikrit because of the special circumstances of their dispossession.[8] They were evacuated by the Israelis from these two Christian villages on the Lebanese border in November 1948 but were promised that they would be allowed to return when the war ended. That promise has yet to be kept. The villagers who remained in Israel have rebuilt their lives, but they never abandoned their struggle to return to their homes and continue to refer to themselves as "displaced persons." Because they are Maronite Christians, and thus closely associated with the sect in Lebanon, it is difficult to see the villagers of Biram, for example, as being in the same category, with the same political claims, as the Palestinians. Yet they too continue to demand that the Israeli government return them to precisely the places they left: not to a neighboring village, not to alternative housing, but to Biram alone.

There has never been anything abstract about the longings of the Palestinians. The object of their longing has always been well defined: the places that had been left behind. For these places were, and to some degree still are, the dominant component of the Palestinian identity. The Arabs of Palestine were never distinguished by a language, a religion, or historical memories of their own. None of these features set them apart from the rest of the "great Arab nation" that extends "from the rolling ocean to the roiling gulf" (in the words of Ahmed Said, Egypt's best-known radio announcer during Nasser's time). The sense of shared destiny that the villagers and city dwellers of Palestine felt toward their fellow Arabs in the country and with the "great Arab nation" as a whole, was vague compared with their strong devotion to the members of their village and clan. The scholar Fawaz Turki, who in 1948 was a child living in the town of Balad Esh Sheikh (on the outskirts of Haifa), claims that he had no sense of being a Palestinian until he fled with his family to Beirut.[9] It was there that the Lebanese would point to him and call him a Palestinian. In a sense every one of the Palestinian refugees was, and remains, a native of Faluja or Jaffa or Sataf or Abassiya. His special attachment to the dunes of Isdud, the citrus groves of Zarnuqa, or the terraces of Saris are of greater importance to him than any other ties. Allegiances of this kind are typical of a conservative society in which the inhabitants of each village have a distinct tradition and blood ties, usually augmented by a special dialect.

Often Israelis have difficulty understanding these components of the Palestinian identity. Under similar circumstances groups of Jews were also left homeless by the 1948 war, as well as by its long prelude. This is not a reference to the members of agricultural settlements like the Etzion Bloc, Atarot, and Kfar Darom, which had been inhabited for only a few years, but to the members of old, established communities such as the Jewish Quarter of Jerusalem and of Hebron. They, too, were dispossessed, but the State of Israel did not look upon them as refugees, and they did not nurture powerful dreams of returning to their ancestral homes and property. The Jew had a different order of priorities. No Jew can be a refugee in the land or the State of Israel. The dominant components of his identity are sovereignty in the land of his forefathers, the Hebrew language, and collective historical memories, not an attachment to a specific house or address. The society of Jewish immigrants in the land of Israel forged a specific, separate identity that is fundamentally different from that of the Palestinians, and the status of the Hebrew language can serve as a good example of how and why it came about.

In the resurrection of Hebrew—one of the most im-

pressive achievements of the Zionist movement and a
key element in the building of the Israeli identity—the
language itself became a kind of homeland for many
Israelis. Nowhere else in the world do people speak and
write in Hebrew. A man whose mother tongue is Hebrew will always feels like a stranger anywhere outside
the State of Israel. The same cannot be said about Arabic for the Palestinians, since it does not differentiate
them as a people. Much to the contrary, it binds them
to the hundreds of millions of Arabs around them, blur-
ring their uniqueness. At the same time, the language
can also be an isolating factor. When its idioms are special, they relate to a specific area, status (urban, rural,
Bedouin), or village, not to the country as a whole.
Palestinian villagers speak dialects different from the
country's Bedouin or city dwellers. In contrast to the
pan-Arab sharing of a language, these local dialects
contribute to a sense of alienation. Thus the woman
from Sataf spoke a dialect unique to the villagers of her
area, who changed the "ch" sound into "ts." Dialects
can even differ from one clan to the next, to the point
where outsiders are sometimes amazed by the fact that
Arabs can identify a man's birthplace or background,
with almost complete certainty, on the basis of his
speech—much as Professor Higgins was able to pin-
point the origins of Eliza Doolittle.

So when the Palestinian refugees dreamed of the
"house over the border,"[10] they dreamed of very distinct places, of "Acre my homeland,"[11] or of Sheikh
Muwannis, or of Birwa; of a specific house (which in
the case of the homeless of Biram and Ikrit isn't even
over the border). The political frontier is of no conse-
quence to them; they are interested only in the fact that
they are not in their homes. "We children in Haifa knew

more about the villages of Scotland than we knew about the villages of the Galilee,"[12] recalled Emil Habibi, a writer and member of the Israel Communist party who studied in the Anglican School in Haifa during the British Mandate. What kind of national solidarity can be built when love of the homeland relates to a single house, perhaps a single village, while a sense of strangeness alienates a man from other neighborhoods, other villages?

The traditional pattern of "local" allegiance became an important strength of the Palestinian struggle after 1948. Constantine Zurayek, a Lebanese intellectual, argues that during World War II a devotion of this kind to land and home forged the morale of an entire people —the Russian people—who fought to defend their homes more than to defend a doctrine, party, or regime.[13] Ironically, however, in 1948 the strong attachment of Palestine's Arabs to their homes and villages was also the source of their greatest weakness. In the absence of broad national solidarity, the Palestinians did not know what to do in order to defend their homes and families. They were torn between the choice of cooperating with the fighters—most of whom were foreign volunteers—or avoiding the struggle, working to arrive at partial settlements, even surrendering to the Jews if only their homes and property would be spared. This dilemma disrupted their struggle and considerably weakened it.

Having been subject to British (foreign) rule, being able to remember Turkish (semiforeign) rule, many of the Arabs of Palestine were able to consider the possibility of Jewish rule. Political regimes were ephemeral in their eyes; the centuries of living on their land were far more compelling than shifting political sovereignties. Many years later, after the 1967 war, the mayor of Hebron, Muhammad Ali al-Ja'abari, remarked, "When I was born the Turks ruled here. I grew up under the English regime, I was mayor under the authority of an Egyptian military governor [in 1948]. Then I took part in the Jordanian regime—and now the Israelis [are here]." Five different political regimes in the life of one man. Each came and went, but Sheikh Ja'abari was still firmly ensconced in Hebron.

Hardly any of the Arabs who left the country in 1948 did so in an organized manner. They regarded their absence, whether they fled or were expelled, as a temporary affair. Often they fled impetuously, in the fear of the moment. Khalil Sakakini, a well-known Palestinian educator, recorded in his diary that neighbors in Jerusalem's Katamon quarter told him of their decision to leave for a while and asked him to keep an eye on their house and some of their belongings. He agreed but eventually fled himself, abandoning his own home, with its large library and all its furniture, as well as the property that had been entrusted to him for safekeeping.[14] In one of Abdul-Hamid Inshasi's stories, the head of the household, Abu Hamdan, urges his wife on the morning of their flight:

> Hurry up, hurry up! We have to leave the house quickly. . . . Tie up only the light things, blankets and some underwear . . . and follow me with the children. Hurry! We'll eat breakfast afterward, on the way. . . . Take bottles of water with you. . . . Put the money in the baby's blanket . . . and put [the gold jewelry] under the hat.[15]

No one thought he was about to part with his home and belongings—to say nothing of his land and its produce. The family of Ghassan Kanafani, the best known of the refugee writers, left their home in Jaffa for Acre in the spring of 1948. But as a boy Kanafani didn't see anything unusual about that; his family visited relatives outside of Jaffa every spring and summer. It wasn't until weeks later, when they fled from Acre to Lebanon, that he realized what had happened. As they sat by the roadside near the Lebanese town of Sidon, his father smiled calmly as he explained that on May 15, when the British leave Palestine, the Arab armies would enter the country, and the entire family would return in the wake of the victors.[16]

According to the oral and written testimony of Palestinians, as well as independent sources in Israel, the Arabs tried to return to their homes almost as soon as they had left them. The Israeli authorities in Jaffa began receiving requests from Arabs to return to the city eight weeks after it had been practically deserted.[17] A few days after abandoning the village of Kheriya east of Jaffa, at the end of April 1948, the village's inhabitants sent the Israelis a message saying that they wanted to come back and were willing to accept the authority of the Jews. The inhabitants of the large village of Zarnuqa south of Jaffa had enjoyed neighborly relations with the Jews of Rehovot and did not flee. However, at the end of May 1948, after the Egyptian invasion of Israel and the threat to the new country's very existence, the local IDF commanders decided to expel them. Zarnuqa's inhabitants were ordered to make their way southward toward the Arab town of Yibne, which was in the path of the advancing Egyptian army. They were terrified, for their good relations with the Jews had made them hateful in the eyes of Yibne's nationalist leadership. Still, their request to remain in Zarnuqa was turned down, and given no choice they abandoned it. Their reception in Yibne was indeed hostile, and when they were banished from the town, they returned to Zarnuqa. But the IDF was determined to keep them out and promptly expelled them again.[18]

The sight of confused Arab refugees torn between their devotion to their homes and loyalty to the Arab cause was a common one throughout Palestine in 1948. At the height of the fighting, many Palestinians who had fled from their homes returned to harvest their fields or pick the fruit in their orchards. At the beginning of June, during the first truce, a government-appointed committee called for giving the army clear-cut orders to prevent villagers from bringing in their crops.[19] Nevertheless, some Arabs—such as the inhabitants of Mailya in the western Galilee—actually managed to return to their villages and remain there.[20]

The wanderings of the refugees through Palestine in 1948 can perhaps be compared to the trek of the refugees through Lebanon during the long civil war of the 1970s and 1980s. During that war terrified people fled first from the southern part of the country to Beirut and from there to the mountains, only to return to the south again; they fled in fear from area to area, but they always yearned for their houses. The Arabs of Palestine had had a taste of flight in the 1936–1939 riots (known to the Palestinians as the Great Arab Revolt), when some left their homes and tens of thousands even fled abroad, including many members of the Palestinian political establishment.[21] In the end, however, almost all of them returned.

It would seem that had the Israeli authorities not prevented it, many, perhaps even most, of the refugees would have returned to their homes when the fighting abated in 1948–1949. In his stories Emil Habibi describes how masses of refugees tried to move back into their villages toward the end of the war, while the Israelis lay in wait for them, catching them and driving them out each time they tried to return.[22] In typically sarcastic language he tells how the Israeli soldiers drove the refugees into the mine fields that had been laid by the British, the Arabs, and the Jews in the Jenin Valley, and how the refugees came back to try their luck again: hiding in fields and in ruins while waiting for night; being nabbed and driven back into the mine fields; making yet another attempt, over and over in an unending cycle that goes on "to this very day," in Habibi's words.

The Arabs of Palestine could not conduct a determined struggle while so many of them, individuals and whole groups, were prepared to compromise with the enemy, to accept his conditions and his rule—if only their land and homes would be saved. And that remained true for many years. Eliyahu Sasson, one of Israel's representatives to the 1949 Lausanne Conference, reported that Arab acquaintances, both private parties and local leaders, tried to reach private understandings with him about returning to the country.[23] The few who succeeded had promised to throw in their lot with the State of Israel, to accept the authority of the Jewish state, and they were permitted to go home. Thirty-five years later, between 1985 and 1984, when Israel invaded Lebanon and took control of the Palestinians living in the refugee camps, many of them pleaded with the soldiers to let them come back to their homes. "We'll do anything," they said, "if only we can return."

3

THE LOST
PARADISE

After the 1948 war the Palestinian refugees were forced to come to terms with the unbearable burden of exile, even though for many of them this exile was in their native land and among their own people. They saw their exile as being "scandalous," "disgraceful," insulting," "degrading," and "humiliating"—adjectives that constantly recur in the descriptions of their feelings.

"Go back where you came from," Lebanese youngsters taunted the children of the Palestinian refugees on the outskirts of Beirut. "You sons of bitches sold your land to the Jews!"[1] Even the dead were scorned in the refugee camps. "These days anyone who dies in our camp qualifies for only four mourners. We're forbidden to congregate," explains one of the characters in a story by Mahmoud Abbasi. "It's bad enough that a man dies in exile, unwillingly. . . . [But on top of that] there's no one to escort him on his way to meet his maker."[2]

Almost as a way of denying their exile, refugee families zealously guarded the keys to their houses [probably already nonexistent) and the deeds to their land, like outcasts who cling to the memory of stolen honor. Visitors to the camps told of the refugees' reverence for any and every document that attested to their association with lost homes: identification cards from the period of the British Mandate, leases, certificates of appointment as a *mukhtar*, business licenses. They held on to these documents as though they might need them at any moment. And even if not, at least they proved that the owners were not merely derelict nomads but people with status and rights, the owners of houses and property. A journalist who asked a refugee family to loan him these documents so that he could copy them was initially refused and finally received them only when he agreed that a member of the family could accompany him to the photocopying shop.

In their incessant yearnings the refugees glorified every detail of the places from which they had been cast out, their "lost paradise." In a protracted pageant of saccharine nostalgia, they spoke and wrote in compulsive detail of every tree, every stone wall, every grave, house, mosque, street, and square they had left behind. "The pomegranates that grew on the tree in Uncle Hassan's yard were the sweetest and juiciest in all the land," wrote Abbasi.[3] Precisely that pomegranate tree and no other. In a TV documentary made in the Aqbat Jabber refugee camp near Jericho in 1988, forty years after the start of the exile, one could still hear the older refugees making statements like: "The motor in my orchards was particularly powerful, twenty-five-horsepower" (an old man from Saffuriya, near Ramle); "In the whole of Kafr Ana there wasn't a single house as spacious as ours" (a woman who left the village when she was still a child).[4] "In our village of Ein Azrab the water was so pure and healthy," a woman from the Deheishe refugee camp confided to writer David Grossman, "that when a dying man walked into it, took a few sips, and washed himself, he was cured immediately."[5]

Traveling along the Jerusalem–Tel Aviv highway at the end of the summer, one can see Arabs harvesting olives by the road near Sha'ar Hagai (Bab el-Wad) at the entrance to the Judean Mountains. They used to live in the now-destroyed villages of the area—Beit Mahsir, Deir Aiyub, and Beit Tul—and still come from afar to harvest the olives from trees that were once theirs. They do so, not as a political statement nor as a symbolic ritual of return, but simply because to them these trees —their olives and no others—are the best in the world. Touching the trees dissolves some of the shame of their lives as refugees, for as the Palestinian peasant saying goes: "What has a man but his God in heaven above and his land on the earth below?"[6]

Only occasionally does this almost-crazed glorification meet with a response of cynicism or contempt among Palestinians. The detailed renditions of the wealth lost by refugee families, or the huge orchards they once owned, have been known to elicit wry comments. Some refugees have ventured that there couldn't possibly have been so many orchards in their homeland unless they were stacked one on top of the other. One poignant story concerns a refugee who visited Israel and found his family's home in a Jaffa suburb. Having borne vague memories of the old house and been raised on stories of the wonderful palace the family left behind, he was appalled to find a small, pathetic-looking building. "Is this what I yearned for?" he asked sarcastically as he stood before the ravaged building. "This ruin is what we're still dreaming of?" [7]

Such apocryphal stories are spread by word of mouth, however; they never find legitimization in Palestinian writings. The same is true of parallel stories in the Zionist canon. One has to do with Yitzhak Ben-Zvi, a leader of the Labor movement, Israel's second president, and an enthusiastic scholar of ancient and remote Jewish communities. He was excited to discover that a Jewish family, the Zeynatis, was living in the Arab village of Peki'in (al-Buqei'a) in the Galilee. According to Zionist myth, they were the only Jews who had remained in the land of Israel throughout the 2,000 years of exile. Ben-Zvi persuaded Chaim Weizmann, Israel's first president, to accompany him to the village and meet this remarkable family. With great difficulty the two men reached the remote, hilly area and made their way through Peki'in, which had fallen into neglect and, like so many other Arab villages, lacked roads, electricity, running water, and all the other amenities of modern life. The Zeynati family, like their Arab neighbors, lived in the most primitive conditions, without sanitation, and in close proximity to their domestic animals. Upon leaving the village, Ben-Zvi bubbled over with enthusiasm, but Weizmann countered soberly: "You know, Ben-Zvi, we were lucky to have gone into exile. Otherwise we'd look and be living like that family."

Cynicism of that sort was hardly ever voiced by the Palestinian refugees. Instead, they aired erotic metaphors of everlasting love and eternal ties to the land of

the village of their birth. Raja Shehadeh, a lawyer from
the West Bank city of Ramallah whose family lost considerable property in Jaffa in 1948, claims that his love
for the land is rife with pornographic feeling. He wan-
ders over the hills, savoring the scent of thyme and the
feel of the hard soil under his feet, and catches himself
gazing at length at an olive tree. The suffering of the
land being taken over by foreigners (Jews), with the aid
of bulldozers, arouses such intense feelings of jealousy
in him that he defines himself as the country's pornog-
rapher. The experience of loss taking place before his
eyes is the root of this powerful sensation.[8] The scent
of the land in the countryside, the embrace of the
fig and mulberry trees, the stubborn adhesion to the
land—these motifs appear in almost all Palestinian
literature, from the abstract love poems of Jabra Ibrahim
Jabra, who hails from Bethlehem and is one of the great
philosophers of the Arab world, to the works of the
young storyteller Akram Haniyeh, the son of refugees
from Abu Shusha and a leading activist in the PLO.

Literary critics describe Jabra's poems about his love
for women and for Palestine as a single blend of mystic love, a divine truth with which the poet seeks to
merge.[9] In everyday life Palestinian expressions of love
are more direct. The mourning mother of a Palestinian
youth killed in the struggle against the Israeli authorities mourns her son as having wed the homeland of
Palestine in his death. This young man who never knew
a woman has sanctified the land with his blood, just as
a young man sanctifies his bride with virginal blood on
their wedding day. The Israelis fostered the concept of
"knowing the land" (knowing in the biblical sense of
the verb), and one of their poets, Alexander Pen, has

written: "O land, my land, I have wed thee in blood." Similarly, and even more intensely, Palestinians project the idea of erotic love onto the peasant's love for his land, his village, and his field.

It was no mere coincidence that the symbolic declaration of Palestinian independence in November 1987 was heralded in leaflets bearing the headline "The Wedding of Palestine." In a traditional society, where blood ties are the backbone of the social structure, the repetition of motifs of erotic geography is readily understood. The soil of the homeland is the object of love, it is both spiritual and material, and it is manifested in the Palestinian's identity.

4

THE OBLIGATION
TO REMEMBER

Since the 1948 refugees were tightly bound to their traditional frameworks, the members of extended families, or clans, tended to remain close, helping each other with funds and housing and looking out for one another's welfare as they had done in the villages and towns they left behind. Major research on the refugees done at Bir-Zeit University from 1984 on has examined where the residents of each village fled in 1948 and where they were located today. Up until now only thirty-five out of a total of 450 villages have been investigated, and monographs have been published on seven of them: Ein Haud, on the southern Carmel range; Lajjun, near Megiddo in the Jezreel Valley; Salama, near Jaffa; Magdal Asqalan, today Ashkelon; Faluja, west of Kiryat Gat in the northern Negev Desert; Innaba, east of Ramle; and Deir Yasin, in western Jerusalem.[1] The prime finding of this research is that the Palestinians who left their homes in 1948 moved to

nearby Arab-held areas, where many of them remained. Thus refugees from the Galilee made their way
to Lebanon and Syria (with a few relocating in the Jenin
District in the West Bank); refugees from the center of
the country went to Nablus, Tulkarem, Ramallah, and
East Jerusalem; and those from the south turned to
Gaza and the Hebron Mountains. For example, most of
the inhabitants of Salama (today Kfar Shalem, in southern Tel Aviv) relocated around Ramallah. Forty years
later about 30 percent of them were still living in that
area, while most of the rest were scattered east of the
Jordan and throughout the Arab oil states. Most of
the urban refugees, almost all of them Christians, and
the members of the propertied classes from the villages
never entered refugee camps at all. Instead, they rented
houses in the suburbs of Gaza, Nablus, Beirut, or Damascus. But they too maintained ties with the past, especially through their clans.

The leading factor in preserving the social structure
and forms of social relations was and remains blood
ties. In exile the refugees continued to marry within
their clans (for the most part to cousins), as well as to
aid the family and to benefit from its economic support.
Even the dialects unique to their places of origin were
kept alive. For some of the refugees the traditional social structure of the clan was undermined in exile, but
for others it was clearly reinforced by participating in
family events such as weddings and funerals. Research
done by Adnan Abdul-Razzeq at the Hebrew University's School of Social Work in 1977 confirmed that family ties were strictly maintained among the refugee
population for over thirty years.[2] Conducted in the Ka-
landia refugee camp on the Jerusalem-Ramallah road,

Razzeq's research focused on twenty families from the village of Saris (today Shoevah, off the Jerusalem–Tel Aviv highway) and showed that, to one degree or another, the broad network of family ties helped his subjects cope with the stress of daily life as refugees. While genuine help was not always forthcoming from various households, the family inevitably closed ranks at times of tragedy and celebration. Exile, it appears, did not change the symbols of status and prestige. Families that had been considered prosperous in their native village also thrived in their new places of residence, even though they had lost everything when they were uprooted, while indigent or otherwise unfortunate families remained equally hapless in their new homes.

Some of the 1948 refugees belonged to families that had been living in cities included within the bounds of Israel—such as Jaffa and Haifa—but originally hailed from two places in the West Bank or Gaza. One was the family of Bulus Shehadeh of Ramallah, founder of the *Marat ash-Sharq* "Eastern Times" newspaper in the 1920s. Shehadeh's sons, Aziz and Fuad, opened a large law office in Jaffa during the British Mandate and acquired extensive property in the city, only to return to Ramallah in 1948. Another is the family of Salah Khalaf (Abu Iyad) the number-two man in the PLO hierarchy until his assassination in Tunis just prior to the outbreak of the 1991 Gulf War. Khalaf's father left Gaza for Jaffa in the 1920s and opened a grocery at the edge of the Manshiyeh Quarter (bordering on what is today Tel Aviv's Carmel Market), but the family returned to Gaza in 1948. Like all the other refugees, these two families lost everything they had in 1948. Unlike many others, however, they were absorbed with relative ease by their native clans. Salah Khalaf tried to obscure this fact when he recalled, with dread, the events of May 13, 1948, when his family fled from Jaffa harbor; he was fifteen years old when his family went into exile. After recounting the horrors of that day, he added: "From that day on, I was destined never to see my home again. Thirty years have passed since then, and I don't know whether the house in which I was born has been destroyed or not . . . and frankly I prefer not to know."[3] Although Khalaf bore the feelings and memories of a refugee "without a homeland" (the title of his book), it is difficult to say that he truly represented the authentic refugee experience. For he and his family were not treated as outsiders in Gaza. Admittedly, they found living conditions among their relatives difficult, but the large clan in Gaza was kin, not strangers. Khalaf's political consciousness, the shame of his bitter personal experience, and a sense of common destiny with the other refugees are what made him into a man "without a homeland." The fate of the refugees who flooded into Gaza and other places where they had no relatives to greet them was far more painful. They did not succeed in becoming integrated. They became true "people of nowhere," displaced persons.

In rural Arab society, it is rare for a family to leave its village and move to another. Usually it is a result of a conflict or to evade the consequences of a blood feud. More often families have moved from villages to cities. But whether a family resettled in the more intimate setting of a village or the more anonymous one of a city, its members were inevitably regarded as strangers in their new surroundings. Anthropologists have concluded that it takes fifty to one hundred years for a family that has moved from one village to another to be absorbed in its new home.[4] The process is complete only when the newcomers establish marital ties with one of the clans in the village. The family becomes part of the economic life of the village and it takes the name of the clan into which it is absorbed. Only then is the family accepted as an integral part of the village—and even then it will often be reminded of its essential foreignness.

As if to illustrate this process, an Israeli-Arab scholar once noted that when he asked a student in Nablus, who had been born and lived in the city, whether his family was a local one—in an attempt to clarify whether he was the son of refugees from 1948—the young man replied, "No, we're not from Nablus. My family came here one hundred fifty years ago."[5] His ancestors had lived in the city for generations, but the student was aware that he still did not fully "belong" in Nablus, and it is fairly certain that the city's veteran families—the "originals," as they are called—still regarded him as something of a parvenu.

If the process of absorbing a single family in a new village was long and hard, the hundreds of thousands of refugees who were displaced in 1948 had virtually no chance of finding their place in new surroundings and being accepted as "locals."

The Palestinian outlook and way of life doomed the refugees of 1948 to remain outsiders and feel like exiles wherever they might go. At the beginning of the 1990s, people in Ramallah and nearby el-Bireh were still able to point out the members of the Tarifi family from the village of Deir Tarif (near Ben Shemen), and the refugee families from Lifta (at the entrance to Jerusalem), for

they continued to be regarded as different, to some degree even as guests, and certainly not as genuinely belonging. Many of the refugee families in Ramallah and
other places built their own small, separate neighborhoods designed to resemble their villages of origin.
Some flourished in business and were able to buy land,
but even their success did not accord them a sense of
truly fitting in, even after more than forty years.

In a number of ways, the sense of exile and alienation
in their new homes has strengthened the refugees' ties
to their villages of origin. Some tacked on to their family
names the names of their destroyed village: Liftawi
(from Lifta), Tarifi (from Deir Tarif), and so on. Others
buried their dead in separate sections of the cemetery
in their new locales. Often the members of a clan, sometimes even if an entire village, know what has become
of every one of the hundreds, sometimes thousands, of
relatives and fellow villagers living in exile east of the
Jordan, in Kuwait, or in the United States. When one of
these distant kin dies, the members of his family and
village gather to mourn him in their new place.

The villagers of Deir Yasin, many of whom have settled on the outskirts of Beitin on the Ramallah-Jericho
road, have preserved their collective identity by pursu-
ing their traditional occupations. Back in their village
they were regarded as experts in quarrying and stonecutting for buildings, and they developed quarries and
stonecutting workshops near Beitin as well. In fact,
they have become successful and prospered, building
lavish homes. They also maintain regular contact with
relatives and other members of the village who have
moved far away. In 1986, when a member of the Deir
Yasin community died in Amman, relatives gathered in

one of the houses near Beitin to mourn. The head of the household in which these second- and third-generation refugees met remarked that if they had been living in Deir Yasin, they probably would not be practicing this custom anymore. But there, in exile, they felt obliged to honor it. Remembering was an obligation, a rite of identity carried over from the past.

In the refugee camps, the consciousness of exile and the maintenance of customs for sustaining the bonds of the clan and original village are naturally far more compelling. These camps are filled mainly by the lower classes of the refugee population, most of them poor peasants or day laborers. They comprise some 850,000 people (according to UNRWA statistics for 1988, thirteen camps in Lebanon with 150,000 people, ten camps in Syria with about 80,000 people, ten camps in Jordan with some 210,000 people; twenty camps in the West Bank with around 100,000 people; and eight camps in Gaza with more than 250,000 people, to which we must add over 50,000 people—again in UNRWA's reckoning —who are living in camps but are not registered in them). The refugees of the camp are, of course, the core of the problem.

In their unrelenting misery, the residents of the camps live on a combination of nostalgia for the past and illusions about the future. Sometimes it seems as though the present is of no import to them, especially in the first and second generation of refugees. When they are not immersed in the past—which has undergone a sea change in their minds—they are living in limbo, waiting for "next year, next time"[6]—be it a war, a peace initiative, an election, a revolution, a convention, a summit, a speech—for inevitably something *must* happen to redress the injustice, set things right, take away their agony, and change the ugly present, which they do not see as legitimate.

This mind-set predisposed the refugees living in the camps to rebel against any attempt to resettle or rehabilitate them. The initiative of King Abdullah of Jordan immediately after the 1948 war sparked demonstrations in the West Bank. When Colonel Husni Zaim (the ruler of Syria for a few months in 1949) broached the possibility of resettling refugees, he was immediately branded as a traitor to the Palestinian cause. The inhabitants of the Hilweh refugee camp near the Lebanese city of Sidon tore up newly planted saplings, for the refugee must oppose anything that accords a camp the least sense of permanence.[7] "I wouldn't live here even in a palace," said an elderly woman who remained in the Aqbat Jabber camp outside Jericho. One of the people standing around her chimed in: "You have to distinguish between a 'resident' and a 'refugee.' The resident lives in his village and on his land; for the refugee, this life is temporary. He can plant a little wheat or raise some vegetables outside his house, but only for now; nothing is done for the more distant future."[8] Otherwise he may prejudice his right to the land of his fathers: his roots will be plucked up; his identity undermined.

The large Jebalya refugee camp in the northern Gaza Strip is populated by the residents of dozens of villages that used to exist on the broad coastal plain south of Jaffa. When one young woman came of marrying age in the beginning of the 1980s, her mother demanded that she marry a member of the clan from her native village of Beit Affa, a village that no longer existed. If she could not find a clan member, she was to marry someone from a neighboring village. Flouting these demands, the young woman chose a man whose family hailed from the large village of Bashit, which had been located a little over twenty miles from Beit Affa. "It's far away," her mother complained. "If we return, and you don't feel well, and I want to visit you, how can I get there from such a distance?" The younger generation was able to convince the mother to agree to the marriage by telling her that the twenty miles was no longer an obstacle, for her uncle had a taxi that would take her there.[9] They didn't dare tell her, "We will never return to Beit Affa."

An incident illustrating a similar mind-set occurred on the main street of Gaza during the early days of the *intifada*. A Molotov cocktail had been thrown at an Israeli jeep. Within seconds all shopkeepers had closed their shutters, a curfew was declared, and the streets were deserted. On one corner, however, an Israeli officer spotted a barefoot beggar dressed in tatters who seemed bewildered by what was happening around him. The officer approached him and explained, "Everyone's gone home. You must go too. Where is your home?" And in perfect innocence and sincerity the man replied, "My house is in Majdal."[10]

Majdal is now the Israeli town of Ashkelon. It hasn't existed for over forty years. But the beggar automatically gave the answer common to most refugees of his generation: the name of a lost village. That is their identity.

5

THE EXPERIENCE
OF LOSS

I n contrast to the Palestinians, and to the Arabs in
general, Israeli Jews have devoted considerable time
and attention to comparing the respective national
experiences of the two peoples. Indeed, many (mostly
embarrassing) parallels have been drawn between the
national rights of the two sides in the Israeli-Palestinian
dispute: between the exile of the Jews and of the Palestinians, between Jewish and Arab refugees, between
the different meanings of "homeland" and varying perceptions of identity. While such comparisons may lack
value in and of themselves, they have been used with
great skill by politicians and propagandists in often in-
furiating demagogy. From one standpoint, however,
there is great importance in the parallels drawn between the experiences of the two peoples: these parallels may affect patterns of thinking and begin to dictate
the policies of each side. Israel's approach to the Palestinians and the refugee problem has often been deter-

mined by these comparisons and their implications, just as the position of the Palestinians toward the Jews and Israel has often been forged by the parallels that they have drawn. Neither side, it seems, is able to escape them.

In the early, critical stages of the 1948 war the British still ruled the land. In the spring they made preparations for withdrawal. According to the borders of the partition plan adopted by the United Nations on November 29, 1947, some 400,000 Arabs would have come under the rule of the Jewish state. With the onset of fighting between Palestinian and Jewish irregulars, the Arabs proved to be poorly organized and were plagued by internal strife. Under such circumstances, anxieties were readily aroused—some more justified than others—and it wasn't long before they translated into general panic. This was the main reason for the subsequent flight of so many Palestinian Arabs. As early as the winter and spring of 1948, months before the State of Israel was established, thousands of Palestinians from the upper classes fled the cities that had become the front line. This trend puzzled the political and military leaders of the Jewish community,[1] some of whom actually believed that the mass departure was essentially an Arab plot to blacken the name of the Jews![2] Still preoccupied with the political struggle to obtain support for the UN partition resolution, the Jewish leadership was eager to prove not only that partition was feasible but also that the 400,000 Arabs slated to live under a Jewish regime would enjoy conditions of equality and well-being. Some Jewish leaders thought that the Arabs were deliberately fleeing as a way of convincing the world that their vision was an unattainable one—that Arabs could not live in a Jewish state—for the

Palestinians had summarily rejected the idea of partition.

In April 1948, after the Arabs of Haifa had left the city in droves, David Ben-Gurion delivered an address before the People's Council (Israel's parliament in the making) implying that he was baffled by the flight. Up to that stage of the war, he noted, not a single Jewish settlement had been abandoned, yet the Arabs had already left some 100 cities, towns, and villages. He also noted that the Arabs were leaving precipitously, after the first defeat, even when they did not face the risk of ruin or slaughter, and he claimed that this proved which of the two peoples was more attached to the land.[3]

"Hey, look over there! They're already running!" says Shmulik in S. Yizhar's short story *"Khirbet Hizah"* as he and his friends approach a village. "Fleeing already? So quickly? Without a single shot?" The young Israeli fighters are surprised. " 'Running, running,' says Moishe. 'They've hooked up their wagons, and loaded their camels, and they're running. Bastards . . . They don't have the guts to fight.' "[4]

The amazement over why these people fled so quickly was shared by the Arabs themselves. Many Palestinians have tried to explain the phenomenon by pointing out the primacy of traditional family ties over an attachment to the land. "We're mad. We didn't have to flee," a young woman tells her elderly father-in-law in a story by Rashad Abu Shawwar, to which the old man replies: "Honor is precious, woman. Would we have left our daughters to the Jews.?"[5] His answer sheds light on the tragic dilemma in which the Arabs of Palestine were caught. The flight from their homes and lands, and all the humiliation it entailed, often stemmed from a fear of even greater humiliation: the desecration of the family and its honor.

The sight of the abandonment-flight-expulsion of hundreds of thousands of Arabs, which Palestinians have described at length, has been documented by relatively few Israelis. One of the most sensitive of these rare descriptions is by Shmaryahu Gutman of Kibbutz Na'an, who was involved in the mass expulsion of the Arabs of Ramle and Lydda and published his account of the operation shortly thereafter in *Mibifnim* ("From Within"), an in-house publication of the United Kibbutz Movement *(Hakibbutz Hameuchad)*, under the pen name Avi-Yiftach:

> Masses of people marched one behind the next. Women bore bundles and sacks on their heads; mothers dragged children after them. Old and young, women and children marched. Many were young men who could have been fighting in the army; they, too, went into exile. Loaded carts were drawn by animals; hundreds of carts, dozens of carts being drawn not by donkeys but by people. There wasn't a single person who wasn't weighed down by some burden. Even every child carried something: a basket of food, a jug of water, a coffeepot . . . I stood on the mosque and through binoculars I saw the masses of people marching toward the village of Barfilya [today at the edge of the Ben Shemen Park] . . . swirls of dust rising in their wake. From close up it was sad to watch this trek of thousands going into exile. As soon as they left the city, they began to divest themselves of things . . . and the roads were cluttered with the belongings that people had abandoned to make their walk easier. . . . They also led goats, sheep, cows, even chickens. . . .

Following this description of "Lydda going into exile," Avi-Yiftach wrote:

> The sight of the masses of Arab exiles conjured up memories of the Jewish exile. The Arabs were not bound in chains; they were not forcibly expelled; they were not led to concentration camps. They went of their own free will to join their people, out of a fear of remaining on the front. But their fate was one of exile. By the glow of the sunset and the spreading twilight, the question hovered in the air: Do they have their own "Jeremiah" who follows in the wake of the exiles, weeping and keening the lament of their tragedy and their shame?

Thus with all the regret and sadness over the Palestinians' "fate of exile," the Israeli's comparison of this tragedy with the Jewish tragedy of exile serves to cushion the terrible impact of the scene and ease the pain. The Arabs are not bound in chains as were the Jews in their exile to Babylon or the rebels of the Second Temple period and Bar-Kochba's day. "They were not led to concentration camps" (suggesting that the Arab tragedy is not even remotely reminiscent of the Holocaust that befell the Jewish people). Most important of all, they were to join other Arabs, their own people.

The Israelis could identify with thoughts of this kind, for the suffering of exile was deeply imprinted upon them. They had left their homes and native lands to live among "their own people" in the land of Israel. Thus the flight of the Arabs, and even their expulsion, took on an aspect of "reasonability," as if to say that there was no place for Arabs in a Jewish environment and certainly not in a Jewish state. On the contrary, they would be better off living among their own kind. Few

Israeli Jews expressed regret at leaving their native lands in the Diaspora. The Zionist ethos had distanced itself from cries of pain like that of the poet Avot Yeshu-run—"I have changed my name, I have changed my language, I have changed my city." The poet, during lonely nights in his new land, with his new identity, heard his original name, Yehiel Perlmutter, being called. The agonies that accompanied the transition to the land of Zion for Jews from all over the Diaspora were simply repressed. All of Israel's Jews are, to one degree or another, refugees or the children of refugees. They have struggled with all their might to shed their exilic identity, to forget the house on the plains of the Ukraine or in the mellah of Casablanca. The Jews came to the land of Israel not only to build it but also to be built by it: to obtain independence and sovereignty and revive their language. As Yeshayahu Leibowitz described the essence of Zionism: "We're tired of being ruled by the *goyim*."

By thus projecting aspects of their own feelings and identity on the country's Arabs, Israeli Jews are quickly able to conclude that the Palestinians have not suffered such a grave injustice, and that, in fact, their situation is a relatively good one. After all, the Palestinians living in Jordan, Lebanon, Syria, and the West Bank and Gaza (up until 1967) were not subject to foreign rule. They lived under sovereign Arab governments, pursued an Arab way of life, spoke their own language, and practiced their religion. Why, then, should they be bitter? Perhaps their devotion to the "idea of return" was no more than a political strategem?

In Israel one constantly hears the argument that the Arabs have twenty-one states and the Palestinians can choose any one of them, but the Jews have no choice:

they have only one country. It is thinking of this sort that has spawned the idea of "transfer" promoted by the supporters of the Greater Land of Israel movement. It has even created a climate in which the novelist A. B. Yehoshua, a prominent supporter of the dovish left, found himself telling his Israeli-Arab colleague Anton Shammas (in the heat of argument), "If you want your full identity, if you want to live in a country with an independent Palestinian character and original Palestinian culture, get up, pack your things, and move 100 meters eastward into the independent Palestinian state that will come into being alongside Israel."[6] Needless to say, the Arabs of Fasuta—Shammas's native village —cannot possibly begin to fathom such a remark. Why should they leave their homes and their land? They already know that even if they move their belongings 100 meters in any direction they will become "exiles"! And where would they settle in the Palestinian state, when and if it is established in the West Bank? In the Deheishe refugee camp? In the Balata camp? They know what befell the others who moved to the West Bank and Gaza over forty years ago, when these areas were ruled by Arabs with an indigenous Palestinian culture. They remained outsiders, miserable wretches. No, the Arabs of Fasuta are going to stay put, as will the rest of Israel's Arab citizens.

The Israeli reading of the situation dictates political behavior that is radically different from that of the Palestinian Arabs. It was no coincidence that during the withdrawal from the Rafah salient in 1982 (consummating the peace arrangements between Israel and Egypt), it never occurred to any Israeli Jew to continue living in the district that was being turned over to Arab rule. To the Jews, it was far more important to exercise sovereignty than to hold on to a specific house or plot of land. There was great symbolism in the destruction of all the buildings that the Israelis had constructed in the town of Yamit and the surrounding agricultural settlements. The razing of the town was a profound expression of protest, as if to say that not even the houses of Jews could "suffer" the rule of foreigners. Letting bulldozers loose on Yamit was a signal that, notwithstanding the hopes that some of them had expressed, the Jewish settlers would never return to the town. Following this precedent, one can readily speculate that if Israel ever withdraws from the West Bank and Gaza Strip, no Jews will remain there either. A withdrawal may be preceded by riots and other forms of struggle, but in the end even diehards like Rabbi Moshe Levinger will leave places of great historic significance like Hebron—and not just for fear of life under Arab rule. For the Gush Emmunim settlers, whose love of the "land of the fathers" in Judea and Samaria has become a passion, the political independence of the Jews is ten times more important than their stake in settlements like Kiryat Arba and Elon Moreh or even than holy places like the Cave of the Patriarchs in Hebron and Joseph's tomb in Nablus. The value of these places as a home in the homeland can be manifested only under Israeli rule, only when they are part and parcel of the Jewish state.

One can even be so bold as to venture that Israelis will not live in this country at all unless it remains a Jewish state. Otherwise they would feel as if they were living in exile, and if one is doomed to exile it is preferable to live it in New York. On the other hand, Arabs whose homes fall within the bounds of the State of Israel will continue living in them, whereas life in an independent Palestinian state deprived of their homes and land would be exile for them. It is a little-known statistic that since the establishment of Israel hundreds of thousands of Jews have left the country (one estimate has the figure at half a million), while the number of Israeli Arabs who have emigrated comes to barely 10,000.

Almost as soon as independence had been declared, Jews began to understand that the Arabs who had fled or were driven out of the country felt no sense of relief at going to live "among their own people." At the height of the War of Independence, some of the participants in the deliberations of the secretariat of the *Mapam* party, the left wing of the Zionist labor movement, noted that the departure, eviction, and prevention of the return of the Arabs would turn these Arabs into "eternal enemies" of the Zionist enterprise.[7] Moshe Dayan came to a similar pessimistic conclusion a few years later, in the early 1950s, when it was more obvious that the refugee problem was pressing. In April 1956 Ro'i Rotberg, a friend of Dayan's and a member of Kibbutz Nahal Oz by the Gaza Strip, was murdered while working in the fields. Standing at Rotberg's grave, Dayan described a recent visit to Israel's southern border where he could see the crowded refugee camps on the outskirts of Gaza. He noted that every inch of the narrow strip of land was intensely cultivated and well cared for. "How can we complain about the [Arab refugees'] fierce hatred toward us?" he asked. "For eight years they have been sitting in the refugee camps of Gaza while right in front of their eyes we are turning the land and villages in which they and their forefathers dwelled into our own patrimony. . . . We are the generation of settlement, and without cannons and steel helmets we won't be able to plant a tree or build a house."[8] Moshe Dayan understood the refugee experience, and his conclusion that the Jews of Israel were doomed to live by their swords was cause for great dismay.

Similar thoughts about the impossibility of solving the dispute because of the refugee problem were aired by Ezra Danin, an official in Israel's Foreign Ministry who had many contacts with Arabs and specialized in the refugee problem.[9] Before 1948 Danin had a Palestinian friend by the name of Hafez Hamdullah from the West Bank town of Anabta, east of Tulkarem. The two men had owned adjoining citrus orchards on the outskirts of the Israeli town of Hadera, and in 1948, with Hamdullah living over the new border, his orchards became the property of the state. Following the Six-Day War, Ezra Danin went to visit Hamdullah, who was by then aged and bedridden but nevertheless immediately recognized his old friend. "Have you watered the orchard?" was almost the first thing Hamdullah asked. Danin was perturbed by the question and later recalled that he was at a loss for what to say. Hamdullah's orchard had not existed for quite some time; it was now part of the town of Hadera. But after almost twenty years the old man's greatest concern was whether it had been watered, as if for all those years he had believed that he could live and die in peace because his Jewish friend was surely tending his orchard for him. Danin then understood the Arabic saying: "I am oppressed, my land has been stolen." Years later, in fact, on the eve of his own death, he continued to argue vigorously: "Unless [we Israelis] refute the Arabs' claim to the land we supposedly 'stole' from them, we will not be able to make any progress toward solving the Middle East dispute."[10]

When the Arabs, and particularly the Palestinians, drew comparisons from the feelings expressed by the Jews and the position taken by the State of Israel, they came to some rather definitive conclusions of their own. Yehoshafat Harkabi argued in *The Arab Position in the Israeli-Arab Conflict* that the Arabs viewed the Jewish national claim as artificial. They saw the Jews as "outsiders" who were trying to purchase, take over, or otherwise conquer land for themselves. Such a claim was a flagrant injustice from every possible standpoint. The hundreds of Palestinians who have written about the conflict in articles, books, poems, and plays have often contrasted the Arabs' natural, native, concrete right to the land to the Jews' invasion and thievery of the land based on a nebulous 2,000-year-old "historical right." Lacking the bonds of modern national solidarity, the Palestinians were unable to grasp what a social or political construct of that kind implied. Instead they compared Zionism and the Zionists to almost every invader in the history of mankind and of Palestine in particular, especially the Crusaders, to the whites of South Africa, and to imperialists of every stamp. A singularly interesting historical comparison appears in the work of the Palestinian scholar Abdul-Latif Tibawi,[11] who attempted to explain to the Jews that if they wished to reclaim a forgotten legacy, they should not be surprised by the hostile reaction of Palestine's Arabs. The Palestinians, who live in the mountains of historic Judea and Samaria overlooking the coastal plain, could see the invaders coming from the west, in from the sea, just as the ancient Hebrews saw the foreign Sea Peoples—the Philistines—coming to invade the country 3,000 years ago.

Since they regard themselves as the "permanent res-

idents" of the country and the only people with a claim
to it, the Palestinians worded the well-known clause of
their National Covenant (clause 6) to stipulate that "the
Jews who lived permanently in Palestine up to the start
of the Zionist invasion will be regarded as Palestinians. . . ." All the rest are foreigners and will have to
leave. The date set by this clause is the Balfour Declaration of 1917. Few Palestinian political activists were
prepared to accept that Israeli Jews could advance their
own claim to the country, speak of the suffering of their
own exile, and pit their own status as refugees against
the claims of the country's Arabs. Mahmoud Darwish,
for example, berates Israelis who try "to flip the rec-
ord," as he puts it, and compare "the Jewish dream of
return" with the "Palestinian dream of return." He is
furious with the Palestinians who are captivated by the
metaphor that tempts them to see themselves as the
"new Jews" and their movement as "Palestinian Zionism." In his view, parallels of this sort are merely expe-
dients for liberal Israelis, who resort to them like a
murderer using "his victim to protect him from the
agonies of guilt." The liberal Israeli loses sleep, in Darwish's rendering, as long as he is the victor, and each
night he makes a partial confession before his Palestinian victim by saying: "We are similar; I am your tor-
mented brother." Thus even as he continues to occupy
the entire Palestinian homeland, he clears his con-
science "while preserving the identity card of the cry-
baby and managing to keep a monopoly on human
suffering." [12]

Indeed, it is hard for Arabs and Jews to avoid drawing comparisons. And if the second- and third-generation refugees lack personal memories of the village and
the home left behind, it is only natural that their long-

ings for the homeland have become more abstract and symbolic—yearnings that are reminiscent of the Jews' longings for 2,000 years. Both sides, says Meron Benvenisti, "have acquired love [of the land] through the experience of loss." For the Jew this is an ancient experience; for the Arab a fresh one. Both live in a new and painful reality. The Jew has transformed his abstract love into something earthy, palpable, and concrete through the cult of "knowing the land" and settlement and accuses the Arab of neglecting the country and reducing it to waste. The Palestinian Arab has taken the opposite course, moving from the earthy to the symbolic and abstract.[13] Zionism perceived the exile of the Jews as an illegitimate element in the life of the nation, a historic injustice that had to be redressed; the Palestinian national movement is equally unwilling to accept the existence of exile or the unending occupation that has turned the Palestinians into exiles in their own land.

The meeting between the Jewish new immigrant to the land of Israel and the Palestinian trying to hold on to Palestine has become a dialogue of the deaf, each living in a separate world with its own images and implications. One example of how this mutual exclusivity operates is the story of the engineer Muhammad Husseini, who went to Amman during the 1967 war and applied to the Israeli authorities for permission to return to the West Bank as soon as it was over. The Husseini family, a wealthy clan with extensive holdings in Jerusalem whose members have held senior government positions in Palestine since the seventeenth century, has in recent generations generally been regarded as the strongest Muslim-Arab family in the country. Moussa Kazem, Haj Amin, Gamal, and Abdel Kader al-Husseini were all prominent figures during the period of the British Mandate, and Faisal al-Husseini is today accepted (with the approval of the PLO) as the leading local spokesman of the Palestinian cause.

After the Six-Day War the Israeli military government tried to limit the number of Palestinians returning to the occupied territories and especially to East Jerusalem, which was quickly annexed to Israel. When Muhammad Husseini received permission to return to the West Bank, he was issued an Israeli identity card establishing him as a resident of Jericho (where the Husseini family also has holdings). Sometime later he insisted upon receiving a document attesting that he was a resident of Jerusalem, where he in fact makes his home.[14] The State of Israel refused to comply, for Israeli officials had been given clear instructions to reduce as much as possible the number of Arabs carrying Israeli documents identifying them as residents of Jerusalem. Muhammad Husseini approached a senior official in the Interior Ministry, a Jew of Polish origin, and explained that he was a bona fide resident of Jerusalem. The official looked at his papers and pronounced: "You are not a Jerusalemite." The astonished Husseini replied: "If I am not a Jerusalemite, who is? You?"

"Yes, me," the official declared, "and *you* are not."

The declaration on the part of the Jew from Poland stemmed from an absolute sense of belonging to Jerusalem, to which he had come (or returned) from a long exile. He did not understand why the Arab standing in front of him was so astonished and outraged. Husseini, whose home and heritage were closely bound to Jerusalem, considered the clerk's statement to be the impudence of a newcomer who was already pretending to be a "local" driving "foreigners" out.

6

A TICKET
HOME

Within a few years of the 1948 war, the Palestinians' sense of exile had become the norm in their society. A way of life emerged that forged a new national consciousness. This was especially true in the large concentrations of Palestinians in the Gaza Strip and Lebanon. Not only were they denied civil rights in these places but they were also taunted and rejected by the surrounding communities.

The Gaza Strip is a short, narrow patch of territory in which employment opportunities were (and remain) highly limited. Once the Egyptians (who controlled the area after the 1948 war) had restricted the free movement of its residents, Gaza became a remote island of humanity, sealed off and suffocating. The 70,000 people who had lived there before the 1948 conflict were literally swamped by some 200,000 refugees, most of them unemployed, forced to crowd into makeshift refugee camps, and living on the dole from the United Nations.

When the 1948 war drew to an end, a symbolic Palestinian government was formed in Gaza under the protection of the Egyptian regime, but it feel soon thereafter. In Lebanon the Palestinians were rejected by the native population because their presence jeopardized the country's precarious balance between rival religious sects. Most of the Palestinians were Sunni Muslims, while the positions of power and influence in Lebanon were held by Maronite Christians, who even then, in the late 1940s, were struggling to maintain their supremacy in the face of pressures from other sects. The economic conditions in Lebanon, which was open to Western influences, had a meliorative effect on the Palestinians there. But like the refugees in Gaza, they felt they had been reduced from "being a people to being a condition," as one of them put it; from individuals with names and a personal status to a blurred, collective visage—in short, to a problem. Rather than being known as Abu Daoud of Mansoura in the Galilee or Abu Ahmed from Brier in the south, they had become the problematic "refugee" in Gaza or the irksome "Palestinian" in Lebanon. It was as though their personal identities had been obliterated. Like the thousands of Armenian refugees from Turkey who had come to the area decades earlier, they were nameless exiles. "Go to the Armenian's shop," people would say—it could be just any Armenian. Now there was a new category: just a Palestinian, a refugee.

At the beginning of the 1960s a number of Palestinian students living in Beirut decided that they could no longer bear this "condition," including the corrupting influence of Western culture. Before the outbreak of the Lebanese civil war, Beirut was flourishing, with a lively commercial, cultural, and social life and a thriving press. During those years Pan-Arab aspirations had been aroused in the Arab world under the leadership of Egyptian President Gamal Abdel Nasser. To preserve their Palestinian-Arab identity, the refugee students in Beirut decided to introduce a radical change in their way of life. One of the students involved, Fawaz Turki, reported that first they stopped using foreign words, a Levantine affectation of which the Maronite-Christian students in Sheikh Pierre Gemayel's Phalangist movement were particularly fond. Then they decided not to patronize any café bearing a foreign name, such as "Uncle Sam" and "Queen's," restricting themselves solely to places with Arabic names like "Fesial's" and "Khalil's." They also placed a ban on listening to Western music. Their adoption of this new life-style went smoothly. They did not draw attention to themselves until it came to the issue of dress. After much deliberation, the main principle won out, and the Palestinian students traded in their jeans, corduroy pants, and T-shirts for traditional clothing from their native villages, clothing collected among the older generation in their families. When they appeared in Beirut's American University dressed in a *jellabiya* (robe) topped by a *kuffieh* and *akal* (headdress), the Lebanese students all but gawked at them in amazement and scorn. " 'O la la,' they would say in French. 'C'est drôle, c'est bien drôle!' " Even Fawaz Turki's father looked at his son "as if [he] were crazy." The intention of these young Palestinians had been to cultivate their uniqueness and prepare themselves to return to their homes and their heritage.[1] The tiny area of Palestine had never been too small to contain the refugees—the poet Mahmoud al-Hout, a native of Jaffa and graduate of the American University in Beirut, wrote at that time—but the entire broad expanse of the Arab world was not large enough to accommodate the exiles.[2]

Episodes of this sort were but one aspect of the creation of an entire culture (literature, poetry, theater) that nurtured the dream of "return." Before 1948 the Arab struggle against Jewish settlement and the British Mandate in Palestine had led the Palestinians only to the point of limited solidarity. After 1948, however, as a result of their exile, about half the Arabs of Palestine had become partners in a clearly defined, painful, and difficult enterprise with a highly concrete aim. Their shared experience bridged social gaps and diminished the antagonisms between economic classes and opposing interest groups, such as city dwellers and country folk, Christians and Muslims, rival clans. Everyone wanted to return. A broad-based and distinctively Palestinian identity emerged for perhaps the first time. "Return" became the common and critical factor that distinguished the Arabs of Palestine from all the other Arab peoples.

The various expressions of this motif utterly dominated the Palestinian cultural vocabulary as far back as the 1950s. Collections of poetry like *Songs of Return* by Ali Hashem Rashid (1960), *Dreams of Return* by Ahmed Fahmy (1957), and *We Shall Return* (1953) by "Abu Salama," the pen name of Abdul-Karem Karame, were published through the early 1960s. In the following years this trickle of books grew into a flood, and there was a concomitant upsurge in the number of stories and nonfiction works offering "a return ticket" (as Nasser al-din al-Nashashibi entitled one of his books), or "the way back," as Yussuf Sibai named his novel. All of these works were of course marked by their "local" flavor and associations. Mahmoud al-Hout wrote of returning to Jaffa, its sea and its orchards; Ahmed Fahmy wrote of Safed and the "regal" Mount Jarmak.[3] Yet the differences between the residents of various villages were superseded by the common desire to return.

This outpouring of feeling bolstered the sense of common destiny that was now shared by all Palestinians, wherever they might be—a sense, as we have seen, that was vague as long as they remained in their land. The inhabitants of the refugee camps developed a strong political consciousness. Their children received a doctrinaire Palestinian education in the UNRWA schools, whose teachers were refugees like themselves, and the new educational system was geared to the experience of the refugee population. (The decisive majority of the UNRWA staff—teachers, officials, welfare and health workers—are refugees, though the agency is run by a handful of foreign personnel.) The clinics, offices, and schools in the camps were decorated with political slogans and scenes of places left behind in Palestine. Maps of the region had Israel painted in black, and in many of the camps the school day began with the children reciting the pledge:

> Palestine is our country,
> To return is our aim.
> Death will not deter us,
> Palestine is ours.
> We shall never forget.
> We shall never accept another homeland!
> Allah and history will attest:
> Palestine is ours,
> And we shall shed our blood for it.[4]

The rite of "return" flourished most of all in Gaza and Lebanon, where the impulse to come out of exile was more powerful due to local conditions. An Egyptian stamp, for example, introduced in the Gaza Strip by Nasser's government, bore the word "returning" and a map of Palestine with a woman gazing wistfully toward it as she held a child in her arms. Everyone in Lebanon seemed to be singing "We Are Returning, We Are Returning," the song of the popular chanteuse Fayrouz, and in every corner one could find the works of the Palestinian artist Ismail Shamout, a refugee from Lydda who had studied in Europe and whose popular drawings on political posters depict the experiences of the refugees longing to return.

Still, the pragmatic outcome of the dreams and the rite of "return" remained limited. In fact, they could easily be dismissed as nostalgic adventurism or an outlet for the buildup of anger and frustration that found expression in metaphors such as "a million exiled slaves who had pledged to return to their homes and become free men." By the end of the 1950s this rite of return had become strident, even pathetic: "The world will hear our marching when we return . . . with thundering storms we will return, with holy lightning dauntless warriors," Kamal Nasser wrote in Beirut in 1960 in a construct typical of its day.[5]

One of the first people to attempt a thorough examination of the refugees' agony was the former superintendent of Arab education in the southern part of Palestine, Abdul-Latif Tibawi, who in 1963 published "Visions of the Return," a detailed analysis of the emotional world of the exiles. Tibawi held that the words, feelings, perceptions, and everything else that went into making the myths and rituals of return were enormously potent elements, the tools of a national mobilization that could actually be more powerful than weapons themselves. The human factor in the peasant's longings to return could not be measured in material terms, Tibawi wrote. Nor could it be summed up as a clear and sharply formulated political consciousness. Instead, the vision of return was, as Tibawi assessed it, a cogent collection of spiritual, even mystic, desires.[6]

The translation of these desires into the language of politics was not long in coming. By the end of the 1950s, while the tensions between the Palestinians and the Arab states continued to rise and fall, a "Palestinian entity" of a patently political nature began to coalesce around the theme of liberation and return. This new "entity" was an attempt to put an end to the situation in which the refugees were being used as a pawn by the Arab states, for ever since 1948 these states had effectively denied the Palestinians a leading role in the struggle for their own country.

Many Palestinian political organizations existed as far back as the late 1950s, but they were barely noticed. They included the Movement for the Liberation of Palestine *(Fatah)* and a number of Pan-Arab nationalist-Marxist groups, the most prominent being the Movement of Arab Nationalists *(Kawamiun al-Arab)*, which held the unity of the Arab world to be a key to liberation and return.

The activists running these organizations were almost exclusively the children of refugees who had been raised in the camps of Gaza or Lebanon and had the experience of exile strongly imprinted upon them. Yasser Arafat, for one, had grown up in Gaza and Egypt.

His two chief deputies, Khalil al-Wazir (Abu Jihad) and Abd al-Fatah Mahmoud, had been born in the vicinity of Ramle and were exiled to Gaza. Salah Khalaf (Abu Iyad), another leading deputy, had been exiled to Gaza from Jaffa; and the brothers Khaled and Hani al-Hassan went from Haifa to Lebanon before moving on to Syria. The Marxist organizations were also built around the sons of refugees, many from the camps in Beirut, including George Habash (originally from Lydda) and the writer Ghassan Kanafani (originally from Jaffa).

One of the PLO's first decisions was to eschew the use of the word "refugees" and replace it with "returnees" (a'idoun). When the organization was established in a meeting in East Jerusalem at the end of May 1964, its chairman, Ahmed Shukeiri, delivered a long address lamenting that "we look out upon our lands and our homes, our houses of worship and landscape, our cities and villages in the stolen homeland."[7] (It may well be no coincidence that in this speech he made reference to Acre, the city of his birth, three times—more than any other place.) In contrast to Gaza and Lebanon, where Palestinian political activity flourished, the largest Palestinian community, in Jordan, responded only partially and weakly to the intensive activity of the Palestinian organizations. In Gaza and Lebanon, however, the Palestinians were struggling for their homes and land, their honor and identity.

In 1964, when the PLO drew up the Palestinian National Covenant, it noted, in article 5: "The Palestinian personality is a permanent and genuine characteristic that does not disappear. It is transferred from fathers to sons."[8] The implication from the outset is that the PLO tried to ensure that both the United Nations and the

Arab states "hosting" the Palestinian refugees would do nothing to resettle them. As one of its resolutions clearly states: "The UN must offer aid to the returnees until the 'stolen homeland' is liberated."[9] Yet the founders' fear that the longing to return would be eclipsed by political plots and schemes seems out of place, at least insofar as the large communities of refugees in Gaza and Lebanon are concerned. Admittedly, even in places where the political and social conditions permitted a degree of integration into the local population (as in Jordan) the Palestinians' efforts to organize on political lines (meaning the founding of the PLO) won at least partial support. In Gaza and Lebanon, however, it yielded more practical results.

Every year the UN General Assembly reaffirms its resolution on the refugees' right of return. And in response to the Israeli government's position that since the Palestinians and the Arab states have brought this tragedy upon themselves it is they who must find a solution to it, Edward Said has written: "The reason for the flight of the Palestinians is not relevant at all. *What matters is that they are entitled to return.*"[10]

7

A VOYAGE
OF DELUSION

The Six-Day War of June 1967 added a new dimension to the problem of "repatriation." Former residents of Jaffa, Sataf, Ramle, and all the other villages, towns, and cities left in 1948 were suddenly able to visit these places after nineteen years. The Israeli conquest of the West Bank and the Gaza Strip, and the subsequent opening of the borders to these areas—as well as to the Arab states via the bridges over the Jordan River—enabled the "people of nowhere" to reestablish contact with "their own place." A twist of historical fate had provided a fantastic voyage of delusion for the refugees who dreamed of an Arab victory that would climax in a homecoming and the restoration of identity through a return to their land, orchards, and wells. Tens of thousands of refugees or more, representing some million and a half others, visited their former lands and homes (or what remained of them). They came out of curiosity, like pilgrims yearning for contact with the house, neighborhood, or village that was to be the interface between their cherished past and coveted future. They went in search not only of houses and orchards but also of forgotten landscapes, old acquaintances, a taste of bygone days, the world of yesteryear.

Many Israelis have told of Arabs suddenly appearing on their doorsteps, looking around, asking questions, and disappearing. This was no "homecoming" but a grotesque distortion of one. Tales made the rounds in post-1967 Israel of refugees coming to search for hoards of gold and silver that had been stashed away in their homes before their flight. One item published in the press[1] told of a seventy-five-year-old woman, Thuriya Makbul, who returned, after the 1971 civil war in Jordan, to her house in Lydda (Lod) to search for a box of jewels she had hidden in the wall. When the Israeli residents of the building refused to let her in, she appealed to the police. The box was eventually found but the woman was not allowed to claim it, for Israeli law classified the jewelry as "absentee property."

One day an Arab appeared at the Jerusalem home of journalist Micha Shagrir, in the Abu Tor neighborhood, and introduced himself as the former owner of the house. After examining the property, he suggested that Shagrir lodge a claim against his neighbor, who, the Arab reported, had encroached upon part of his courtyard and fenced it off. "I am prepared to testify in court that it is ours," the Arab assured him, leaving Shagrir appalled by this declaration of joint ownership. In the town of Azor (formerly the large Arab village of Yazur on the outskirts of Jaffa), a family of Israelis politely welcomed a group of Arabs who had owned the house they now occupied. The two groups spent a Saturday together, with the Arabs reminiscing about the past. The following Saturday the Arabs again visited and chatted with their hosts. When they turned up for the third time, the Israelis felt uneasy and, sensing this, the Arabs said they would sit outside in the street; all they wanted was to gaze at the house and its adjacent garden. On the fourth Saturday, the Israeli family called the police, who drove the Arabs off.

Such visits by former residents often caused consternation among the Israelis. Some of the kibbutzim built near or on the ruins of Arab villages had taken special care to remove all evidence of these settlements after 1967 by plowing over the sites and planting orchards. When the refugees returned to visit their homes, they could find hardly a trace of them.

Like so many other refugees, the al-Khayri family came to see the home in Ramle from which it had been expelled in 1948.[2] Theirs was one of the leading families in Ramle, the only city in Palestine founded by Arabs. During the period of the British Mandate, Mustafa al-Khayri had been mayor of Ramle for a number of years, while another family member, Haluzi al-Khayri, had been the district officer. Bashir al-Khayri was six years old when his family was expelled from Palestine. A lawyer in 1967, he accompanied his elderly parents to see their old home in Ramle, which was inhabited by a Jewish family who had immigrated from Bulgaria. Bashir's father, by then blind, caressed the stones of the house and asked to be taken to the lemon tree in the garden, where he stood and unabashedly wept.

Shortly after that visit Bashir al-Khayri became the leader of a terrorist cell affiliated with the Popular Front for the Liberation of Palestine, headed by George Habash (who hails from nearby Lydda). The members of his cell planted bombs in West Jerusalem, including the cafeteria of the Hebrew University, and Bashir was apprehended, tried, and sentenced to life imprisonment. But in 1985 he was released as part of a prisoner exchange engineered by Ahmed Jibril, the leader of another Palestinian organization. Three years after his release, in January 1988, Bashir al-Khayri was again arrested, this time charged with being one of the organizers of the *intifada*, the Palestinian uprising. On these grounds, he was deported to Lebanon.

But this story has a special coda because of Dalia Landau, who struck up an acquaintance with Bashir al-Khayri. Dalia was a year old in 1948 when her parents moved into the al-Khayri house in Ramle and twenty when Bashir and his parents came to see it. Though she continued to meet with Bashir after that visit, she realized that despite her relatively liberal views she would never find a common language with an activist of the Popular Front, which denies Israel's right to exist. Nevertheless, when Bashir al-Khayri was deported, Dalia Landau published an open letter to him in the *The Jerusalem Post* (January 14, 1988) informing him that her parents had died since they had last met and she was the heir to the house that was the link between them. "I talked over my thoughts about the house with my husband," she wrote to Bashir, "and we decided to dedicate it to a cause that might lead to a solution of our problem. We want to do this in consultation with you."

Of course, no refugee ever got any part of his property back. Israeli law absolutely precludes that. The one notable exception was when refugees from Wadi Fukin came back to rebuild their village in the Jerusalem Corridor. The pre-1967 border ran through the heart of Wadi Fukin and, abandoning the Israeli side, its residents moved eastward to the adjoining areas, where they continued to cultivate their lands inside Jordan. After 1967, however, they slowly filtered back to their ruined houses, rebuilding them and in some cases even constructing new ones.

Usually the refugees returned to their former homes only a few times. For many it was a painful experience. Dr. Sharif Kana'ne, who conducted research on Palestinian refugees at Bir-Zeit University, told of escorting two refugees to the ruined site of the village of Innaba west of Latrun (just off the Jerusalem–Tel Aviv highway). Though hardly anything remained of the place, the two visitors managed to find some indications that this was indeed the site of their village. Nevertheless, the surroundings had changed so radically that one of the refugees stubbornly rejected the evidence, insisting that it was not where Innaba had once stood. Eventually they came upon a small mound of earth with some rocks, thistles, and remnants of simple gravestones. These were the remains of Innaba's cemetery, and as fate would have it one of the surviving headstones bore a faded inscription of the name of none other than the skeptical refugee's father. The man burst into tears. When Dr. Kana'ne asked the two refugees to return to the site with him, they refused. All the money in the world, they said, wouldn't compensate for their pain at seeing their village destroyed.

Perhaps the most vivid description of such renewed contact with lost homes is a fictional account called "Returning to Haifa" by Ghassan Kanafani, one of the best-known works of Palestinian literature.[3] The story tells of a young Arab couple from Haifa who desert their home in April 1948, together with the rest of the city's Arab residents, and in the confusion of flight leave their five-month-old infant behind. In subsequent years they wander from place to place and have more children, but they never forget the child, Khaldun, abandoned in Haifa. After the 1967 war they return to the house in Haifa and find their home exactly as they had left it; even the furnishings remain the same. It is inhabited by a Jewish woman, who greets them by saying: "I've been waiting a long time to meet you." It transpires that the woman is a survivor of the Holocaust whose husband was killed in the 1956 Sinai Campaign. She has a son named Dov who is actually their son Khaldun. The Jewish couple had found him in the house and adopted and raised him. Now the three parents wait for Dov-Khaldun to return and face the decision of whether to remain with his Jewish mother or join his Arab parents. When the twenty-year-old youth, a soldier in the Israeli army, arrives home late that night, he has no problem choosing to remain in Haifa with his Jewish mother. "How could you have left an infant in his crib and fled?" he snaps at his natural parents. "Twenty years have passed, sir! Twenty years! . . . Don't tell me that during those twenty years you wept! Tears will not restore what has been lost."

The allegorical nature of this story is hard to miss. The infant left behind in Haifa is analogous to the homeland abandoned by the Palestinians. The Jews adopted and nurtured it, and now it is loyal to them. "Returning to Haifa" means returning to an open wound, to a pain for which there is no cure other than struggle, opposition, and war. At the end of the tragic encounter in Haifa, Khaldun's father asks his son:

> What is the meaning of homeland? Is it these two armchairs that have remained in the house for twenty years? Is it the table? The peacock feathers? The picture of Jerusalem on the wall? The copper door latch, the oak tree? The balcony? What is the homeland, Khaldun? Our illusions?

His other son, Khaled, who was born in a refugee camp, never even knew the house in Haifa. "What meaning does Palestine have for Khaled?" the distraught man asks his wife. "He recognizes neither the flowerpot nor the painting nor the staircase, neither the neighborhood nor Khaldun." The two refugees came looking for something covered with the dust of memories, and what did they find? More dust. Ghassan Kanafani's story concludes with its two protagonists, the Arab parents, permitting their son Khaled to join the Palestinian guerrillas so that what happened to Khaldun, the Arab who was transformed into Dov the Jew, would not happen again.

The terrible irony is that after 1967 the first generation of refugees realized that their children, though unacquainted with the traditional elements of the homeland, understood the concept of homeland far better than they did. Returning to places that had actually been theirs, the 1948 refugees found that the houses and lands had become unreal. "Their place" had become part of someone else's history. Can the love of a particular house or patch of soil pour content into the Palestinian entity and national identity? Kanafani believed it could not. To do so required much more. The vision of return held by the first generation of refugees seemed rather petty to their progeny, like the whim of a child who had been deprived of a toy. To the younger generations Palestine was of course a place to return to but also an entirely new place, one where general and abstract longings would be fulfilled and not just the solution to the problem of any one refugee or another. And to fulfill these longings, they must fight.

That was the thinking that lay behind the PLO's terrorist and guerrilla activities after the Six-Day War. Immediately after the defeat of the Arab armies in June 1967, the children of the 1948 refugees took it upon themselves to wage a struggle against Israel. Adopting the Algerian model and doctrine of a popular uprising, *Fatah* and other Palestinian organizations went about recruiting youngsters from the refugee camps, especially in Lebanon and Syria, where the response was considerable. The young people underwent hasty military training, with help from the Syrian army, and were sent to the West Bank to organize underground cells and carry out sabotage operations in Israel. In the summer of 1967 Yasser Arafat himself spent several weeks in the West Bank personally supervising the organization of these networks. Within a few months, however, it was clear that the *Fatah* squads operating in the West Bank and East Jerusalem were not winning the support of the local population. The traditional closed social structure worked against their acceptance and, coupled with the villagers' fear of the Israeli reaction, led to their being driven out of the villages. Sheikh Muhammad Ali al-Ja'abari, the mayor of Hebron and one of the most revered leaders in its vicinity, publicly declared that he was prepared to chop off the arm of the youth who had thrown a hand grenade at Israelis in the Tomb of the Patriarchs.

The journalist Ehud Ya'ari investigated the activities of *Fatah* in the West Bank at the end of 1967 and the beginning of 1968. He found that the second-generation refugees who had infiltrated into the area failed to organize an armed uprising there. Essentially, this was because *Fatah* was a product of the Diaspora; it had developed outside of the territories. Its way of life—one of exile in squalid refugee camps—was alien to the people in Nablus, Hebron, and Jenin who had remained on their land.[4] Not a single member of the dozens of *Fatah* squads caught by the Israeli security forces was an indigenous resident of the West Bank. All were the children of refugees from 1948, and it turned out that the *Fatah* members who were killed in terrorist actions all were traced to places that were relatively distant from the West Bank. Perhaps this is why the West Bankers themselves, who were busy trying to adjust to Israeli rule, were unresponsive to the "Heroes of the Return" (as one of the organizations affiliated with the Popular Front for the Liberation of Palestine called itself). Thus as early as 1968 *Fatah* and other Palestinian organizations were gradually forced to move their bases to the East Bank of the Jordan, where they were well received in the large refugee camps. At that time about 300,000 Palestinians who had fled from the territories occupied by Israel in 1967 settled into the established refugee camps on the East Bank, particularly around Amman, creating something of a "state within a state." In Gaza, unlike the West Bank, the PLO enjoyed great success. The inhabitants of the refugee camps joined underground cells in such impressive numbers that in 1969

Arafat was able to boast that while Moshe Dayan might control Gaza during the day, the PLO ruled it at night. Indeed, the Israeli press reported that armed young men circulated quite openly in the refugee camps. The PLO's sway in the Jordanian camps ended with the civil war of 1970–1971 ("Black September"), and at the same time Israel launched a determined military operation to wipe out the organization's cells in Gaza. Thereafter, the PLO moved its headquarters to Lebanon, and after the Yom Kippur War (October 1973) it began to channel its energies into diplomatic efforts. The first generation's dream of return gradually receded. The impossibility of the dreams became increasingly tragic with the passage of time, for they were dreams that could not be realized by force of arms.

During the 1970s the East Jerusalem Palestinian journalist Hana Amira, who had been a mere infant when his family was displaced from Ramle, was arrested by the Israeli security services and sentenced to five years in prison for collaborating with an enemy organization. He was incarcerated in the Ayalon Prison in Ramle, the city of his birth. "Well, what do you want?" he used to ask his visitors cynically. "At least I've come back to Ramle."

8

REFUGEES IN
THEIR HOME

S trange though it may seem, the theme of "return"
also became a key component in the worldview of
those Arabs who remained in Israel and assumed
its citizenship. Yet here the motif acquired a unique
coloration that transformed it into its own opposite: not
actually "returning" at all but staying put, "holding
fast."

When the signing of armistice agreements with the
Arab states in 1949 legally established Israel's borders,
it turned out that some 160,000 Arabs remained within
the new state. Clearly they were a minority—17 percent
of the population—and this proportion of Arabs to Jews
has remained more or less constant in Israel ever since.
In 1989 the country boasted over 600,000 Arab citizens,
with the dramatic growth rate due primarily to natural
increase.

The two large groups of Arabs in Israel were then,
and remain today, in the Galilee (especially its central

and western portions) and the so-called Triangle (bordering on the northern West Bank from Kafr Kassem in the south to Wadi Ara in the north). To these demographic clusters we must add the Bedouin population in the Beersheba region of the Negev and large urban communities in Haifa and Acre together with smaller ones in Jaffa, Lod, and Ramle.

Each of these groups resulted from circumstances that were unique to the respective area during the fighting in 1948.[1] Almost all the Arab villages in the upper Galilee, eastern Galilee, and part of the western Galilee were destroyed, while most of those in the central Galilee, including the two cities of Nazareth and Shefar'am (Shafa'amar), emerged from the fighting intact. Like Haifa, Acre, and the surviving villages in the north, these two Galilean cities were brimming with refugees from the devastated settlements in the area. According to estimates made in the early 1950s, some 20 percent of the Arabs who became Israeli citizens had been displaced from their homes in one way or another. Thus in addition to the tens of thousands of people who had fled into Arab-held territory, thousands of other Arab refugees were to be found within the boundaries of Israel proper. Some of the Arabs who fled from Tiberias, for example, settled in Nazareth, which was likewise the destination of Arabs who fled from the town of Safiriya (Tsippori) and villages in its vicinity. Some of the inhabitants of Birwa (near the Ahihud junction) moved into nearby settlements, and the refugees from Biram and Ikrit established themselves in Ramah and Jish.

Among the villages that remained intact when the fighting had ended were those of the Druze, a sect that had broken with Islam in the eleventh century and lived mostly in the mountains of Syria, Lebanon, and northern Palestine. In the course of the 1948 war, many Druze joined the ranks of the Israeli army. Other Galilean villages had a mixed population composed of various sects, including a relatively high number of Christians, a population that the State of Israel wished to cultivate. It was these villages that proved to be fertile ground for the growth of the Communist movement. Its leaders were for the most part Christian Arabs and its members generally supported the 1947 UN partition resolution. This was contrary to the stand of the mainstream Palestinian leadership and of the surrounding Arab states. Eventually the Communists in the Galilee made common cause with their Jewish comrades in establishing a joint political framework, the Israel Communist party, which made great inroads among the Arabs in Israel.

Unlike its counterpart in the Galilee, the Arab population living along the border with the West Bank was homogeneous in character, being almost entirely Muslim. There are over twenty Arab villages in this sector, and they had come under Israeli control as a result of the armistice agreement with Transjordan, in which King Abdullah found himself forced to cede a three-to-four-kilometer-wide strip from southern Samaria to the outskirts of the Jezreel Valley. This strip had been occupied by Iraqi forces during the 1948 war. When the Iraqis evacuated, the Israelis demanded control over the area, and their demands were met. In other places small knots of Arab settlement were the result of local and occasionally totally random incidents that had occurred during the war. This was the reason that Abu Ghosh in the Jerusalem Corridor and Jasr al-Zarqa and Faradis on the Tel Aviv–Haifa road survived virtually unscathed. Few Arabs remained in Acre, Ramle, Lod, and Jaffa, but those who did were joined by refugees from other places. Due to the trauma of the war and their subsequent isolation from the rest of the Palestinians, the Arabs of Israel found that the process of clarifying their status and special relationships was both a long and a slow one.

For eighteen years, from 1948 to 1966, the Arabs of Israel were subject to the rule of a military government that forbade them to leave their areas of residence without special passes and placed other restrictions on their personal liberties. Large tracts of land were expropriated from them, by means of legislation and administrative fiat, and Jews settled them.[2] Despite these strains, however, the Arabs of Israel were gradually integrated into the country's economic and social life. The powers of the military government were eventually curtailed, and they were abrogated altogether in 1966. The expropriation of land gradually came to an end while the economic status of the community rose appreciably, and the level of services improved in the Arab sector. In theory the Arabs of Israel are citizens with equal rights, though in practice they do not enjoy full equality —especially as the great majority of them do not serve in the military and are thus denied the array of benefits and prerogatives accorded to army veterans.

It was all but inevitable that the social and political circumstances prevailing in Israel would generate a deep, unsettling contradiction in the life of the country's Arab citizens. It found expression in the succinct pronouncement of Abdul-Aziz Zuabi of Nazareth (a deputy minister representing the left-wing *Mapam* party): "My people are at war with my country," which became a haunting refrain that was aired at almost every public discussion of the Israeli-Arab cause. Even the term "Israeli Arab" loses all meaning when Jews and Arabs alike are confused about the application of such terms as "people," "nationality," and "citizenship." Since the very word "Israeli" implies the Jewish identity of the state, the term "Israeli Arab" effectively refers to "Jewish Arab," which in standard Israeli terminology is a contradiction in terms. Neither is the term acceptable to the Arabs as long as they deny the existence of a Jewish nationality and maintain that Judaism is exclusively a religion. Some have argued that the Jews who lived in Arab lands over the centuries are "Jewish Arabs," just as there are "Christian Arabs" throughout the Near East today. Even Yasser Arafat has made this claim. In any event, neither the PLO nor any Arab government has ever spoken of "the Arabs of Israel"; all use the term "the 1948 Arabs" or, in the case of the PLO, the "Palestinians inside."

At least until 1967, the Palestinians in the Diaspora, like most other Arabs, tended to regard their brethren living in Israel as hapless and oppressed people, many of them "Judaized" and "spies," while Israel's Jews generally suspected them of potential, if not inherent, disloyalty. Participating in a conference in Eastern Europe, the poet Rashid Hussein from the village of Mus-mus in Wadi Ara found that the members of the Arab delegations treated him with hostility because, in their perception, he lived in two spheres—that of his Arab identity and that of his Israeli citizenship—when in fact he belonged to neither. In order to "belong" (at least until the late 1970s, and to a certain degree even afterward), the politically conscious Arab had to identify definitively with one side or the other. Thus the jurist Sabri Jiryis from the Galilean village of Fasuta left Israel after the Six-Day War and joined the PLO hierarchy abroad, as did the poet Mahmoud Darwish in 1971. But many took the opposite course. Ever since the first parliamentary elections in 1949, Arab Knesset members have been associated with Zionist parties. There have been Arab employees in government institutions and Arab activists in public organizations and the General Federation of Labor since 1949. Those who identified openly, and even demonstratively, with the institutions of the state earned the epithet "positive Arabs" in Jewish eyes (meaning the adviser for Arab affairs in the prime minister's office), while their opponents in the Arab public sneeringly referred to them as "the tails of the regime." One way or another, most of the Arabs of Israel sensed that both the Arab world and Israel had turned their backs on them.

As we have said, the decisive majority of Israeli Arabs (some 80 percent) remained in their homes and villages in 1948. But they were joined by refugees, and common to both these groups was the fact that they had lost large tracts of land. Like Israeli rule itself, this concrete loss sparked anxieties of losing their personal identity, just as it had among the refugees over the border. "We are particularly interested in the land problem because the land is perceived as a key part of a man's identity," wrote the Israeli-Arab literary scholar George Kanaze[3] in language similar to that of the Palestinian exiles. Indeed, the tie to the land features prominently in many of the public and political activities engaged in by Israeli Arabs. The first time they tried to establish a nationalist party in Israel, they called it *al-Ard* ("The Land"). It grew out of a journal of the same name at the end of the 1950s, and its members tried to register their party as an association in 1964. But the government outlawed their activities as seditious, and the Supreme Court upheld the decision.[4] Since 1976 the Arabs of Israel have institutionalized other ways of expressing their protest, such as the demonstrations held annually on March 30 —known as "Land Day"—and the appointment of a special watch committee called the Committee to Defend the Land. To these examples we can add a long list of commemorative names that attest to the emphasis placed on the bond with the soil of the homeland.

Israel's Arab citizens have also written hundreds, perhaps even thousands, of poems, stories, articles, and plays about this. One of the poems, Mahmoud Darwish's "Identity Card," published in July 1963, has become practically the anthem of the Israeli-Arab community, and almost every schoolchild knows it by heart. It reads, in part:

> *Write:*
> *I am an Arab*
> *I have no title, no name.*
> *Patient am I in a land that lives*
> *In an overflowing of rage. . . .*
> *My father is from the family of the plow,*
> *Not the son of noble lords.*
> *My grandfather was a peasant,*
> *Without lineage or pedigree,*
> *Who taught me the dignity of the soul*
> *Before he taught me to read!*
>
> *Write:*
> *I am an Arab*
> *And the color of my hair . . . is like coal,*
> *And the color of my eyes . . . is brown,*

And my address: I am from a forgotten village
Whose streets have no names. . . .

Write:
I am an Arab.
My ancestors' vineyards have been stolen from me.
Land that I used to work,
I and all my children.
And nothing remains to us . . . and to all my progeny
Other than these stones.
Will your government take them as well? [5]

The poem, written as an Arab's declaration of identity before an official of the Jewish regime, strives to epitomize the Israeli-Arab experience. In contrast to that of the refugees over the border, who were exiled from their land, Darwish's testament flows from the sensibility of a national minority that remained on its land but is subject to the rule of an alien majority. Obviously these two experiences are joined to the same stock of a divided and torn people that aspires to reunite in a land of no longer its own.[6] But there is a substantial difference between them, and it comes out most clearly in the order of priorities adopted by these two branches of the Palestinian people. For the Palestinians who have become refugees, return is the most important thing, almost everything. It is a longing shared by the Christian-Arab aristocrat, the urban Arab who fled from Haifa to Beirut, and the seminomadic Bedouin who was driven from the Negev into the Gaza Strip. The mirror image of flip side of "return," however, was to make tenacity—cleaving to the land in the face of the threats from every quarter—into the essence of a common identity. Reduced to its simplest terms, the difference between the two foci of identity is that the Palestinian outside wants to return, the Palestinian inside is determined to stay.

The ethos of clinging tenaciously to the land, which developed among the Arabs of Israel during the 1950s, was apparently adopted and reinforced after the Six-Day War by Palestinians in the West Bank and Gaza Strip, where it became known by the term *"summud"* ("steadfastness," or "holding fast"). The desire to stay put at home, and on the land, is described in numerous works by Israeli Arabs with an intensity of feeling that matches the refugees' passionate expressions of their longing to return. "Like an oak we shall remain here," wrote the poet Salim Jubran of Peki'in in 1969, "like rocks, like the olive groves on the hills of my country."[7] And the poet Tawfiq Zayyad, a member of the Knesset and mayor of Nazareth, added:

> *It would be easier*
> *To catch fried fish in the Milky Way,*
> *To plow the sea,*
> *To teach the crocodile to speak,*
> *Than to force us to go.*[8]

Before leaving Israel to take up a position in the PLO, even Mahmoud Darwish proclaimed: "A homeland is not a suitcase, and I am not going. I am the lover, and the land the beloved."[9]

These declarations, so characteristic of the corpus of Israeli-Arab writing that later became known as "resistance literature," accompanied a long struggle by the Arabs of Israel to defend the right to their land. On the face of it, they were bewildered by what had befallen them. After all, they had done all the right things. They had stayed put in their villages and become citizens of the state. Why, then, should they be deprived of their property? "Although many inhabitants of our village fled," wrote Arabs from the Galilee in a letter published in the government-sponsored Arabic daily *al-Yom* ("The Day") in December 1950, "we decided to remain under the aegis of an honest and democratic state that advocates freedom and equality. But then suddenly members of the neighboring kibbutz came and seized our fertile coastal lands." "As people who love their land," echoed representatives of Galilean villages at a news conference in Tel Aviv in 1963, "we have remained here . . . and we hope to be treated amicably by the authorities. [But] we have discovered that the opposite is the case. . . . The expropriation of [1,250 acres] of our agricultural land . . . is a blow that strikes at the very essence of our being. . . . Why should we give our land to others?" [10]

The political circumstances forced them to grapple with a cruel paradox: to keep their hold on their homes and lands, they were forced to make concessions. Sometimes it seemed that their devotion to their land was so great that they were willing to pay an extremely high price for it. This set them apart from their brothers over the border and effectively sundered them from the Palestinian identity that was evolving outside the State of Israel. If the motif of "return" required the refugees to wage a relentless war against Israel, the commitment to tenacity called for a struggle of a different kind. It required the Arabs of Israel to take a tortuous path toward integration into the Jewish state, a state born under conditions that made them first into its enemies, then into the "aliens within." In other words, the same "local" quality of belonging to the village, field, and clan that had made the refugees into such wretched outsiders in their places of exile was what prompted the Arabs of Israel to absorb whatever blows the new regime brought down on them, as long as they could avoid being uprooted and losing what remained of their identity.

The Communist party, which defined itself from the outset as a non-Zionist Jewish-Arab framework (although the overwhelming majority of its voters have always been Arabs), made a decisive contribution to this posture by enabling the Arabs of Israel to take part in the state's democratic processes and wage a determined struggle for equality. It dissociated the desire to remain on the land from a willingness to capitulate to the regime, and identified instead with waging a struggle for equal rights within the bounds of Israeli democracy.

9

ARE YOU
SUBLETTING?

J ust as the opening of the borders in 1967 beckoned
the Palestinian refugees onto a voyage of delusion
to homes that were no longer theirs, so it tempted
the Arabs of Israel to embark on an equally fantastic
voyage back to their identity as Palestinians. The writer
Anton Shammas, from the Galilean village of Fasuta,
has described the resumption of contact between the
Arabs of Israel and their Palestinian brethren as an
overdose of oxygen flowing from the other side of the
Green Line (the former border between Israel and the
territories). "After long years of total cultural and social
isolation, they could now feel the special intimacy of
two strangers who suddenly found themselves laugh-
ing at the same joke (in this case a very costly joke)."[1]

Many Israeli Arabs hurried over the Green Line to
visit family and friends, buy bars of olive oil soap in
Nablus, and savor the taste of *knafa,* a local delicacy
made of semolina and sweet cheese that is famous

throughout the Arab world. Others streamed to the holy mosques on the Haram el-Sharif (or Temple Mount) in Jerusalem, while yet others descended upon the bookshops of East Jerusalem, snatching up books and journals that were unobtainable in Israel. Emil Habibi set down his impressions of this dramatic encounter in a series of stories entitled *The Six-Day Sextets*, where the joke that Shammas referred to as "costly" is portrayed more as a bitter one. For beyond being the result of a defeat, rather than a glorious victory, the reunion of Israel's Arabs with their Palestinian kin was only an illusory one and in fact could not bridge the gap between people who were divided by political borders and civic loyalties.

In his critique of Emil Habibi's story "The Almond Tree Finally Blossomed,"[2] the writer and critic Shimon Ballas analyzes the character of an Israeli-Arab teacher who secludes himself in his home from 1948 until 1967. (Needless to say, the fact that he was granted a job as a teacher in the State of Israel automatically makes him suspect in the eyes of his fellow Arabs.) The 1967 war forced him out of his isolation, and he began visiting long-lost friends in the West Bank, which "raised his spirits as well as his standing." The teacher was looking for a childhood friend whose name he had forgotten but who, as a young man, had promised to be faithful to a girl living in the West Bank. The crux of the tale is that the elusive friend was none other than the teacher himself, who had succumbed to a kind of amnesia or schizophrenia. Even when he visits the home of the girl (now a woman), he is unable to recall that in their youth he had promised to marry her. He cannot overcome the split in his personality and remember his love, just as most Israeli Arabs cannot overcome the rift in their souls that results from their being at one and the same time Palestinians and Israelis.

In the years following the 1967 war, when the Palestinian guerrilla organizations gathered strength, their prestige rose considerably in the eyes of many Israeli Arabs. Some young Arabs from the Galilee and the Triangle even joined clandestine cells of the PLO and resolved to commit acts of sabotage. The links created between political organizations in Israel and in the territories[3] also found their reflection in Israeli-Arab literature. In another story by Emil Habibi, a young Arab woman from Haifa who is arrested because of her political activities finds herself imprisoned with a woman from the West Bank. The latter asks her why she likes the song "We Are Returning, We Are Returning" by the singer Fayrouz. After all, she had never been driven off her land or exiled from her home or country. "My country?" the woman from Haifa replies bitterly. "I feel as though I am a refugee in a foreign land."[4] The expressions "refugees in the homeland" and "strangers in the homeland," which come up again and again among Israeli Arabs, bear witness to their state of mind. Yet such feelings have not prompted masses of Israeli Arabs to join the Palestinian national struggle in the territories or abroad. Instead, the Arabs of Israel persisted in their pre-1967 struggle to obtain equal rights in their country, a political struggle waged within the framework of the country's political system so that the Arab citizen could feel less like a stranger in his own land. The by-product of this struggle, however, was that the sharp differentiation between the Israeli Arabs and the Palestinians in the West Bank and Gaza persisted.

Generally, the attitude of Israel's Arabs toward the

Israeli state remained much the same before and after 1967. The members of the community maintained their political activities, voted in the Knesset elections—more or less along the same lines as they had prior to the war —and remained (albeit unequal) partners in the country's public and national life. They did not boycott Israeli governmental bodies, as was frequently the practice among the West Bank Arabs; nor did they demonstratively discard their Israeli identity cards, as the Druze inhabitants of the Golan Heights did when Israeli citizenship was imposed upon them in 1982. To the contrary: though their status rose in the eyes of the Arab world, their sympathy for the Palestinian cause increased, and many of them stressed their national identity as Palestinians. Most Israeli Arabs remained mindful of their unique order of priorities as Israeli citizens—chief of which was the achievement of equality.

Though successive Israeli governments insisted that the Green Line was a matter of history and would never be reinstated, and even after the border had been erased from the official maps, it remained intact for Israeli Arabs. Indeed, it seemed to have been accentuated and reinforced. While both overt and covert nationalist institutions were established jointly in the West Bank and Gaza Strip—national committees, steering committees, the Palestinian National Front,[5] the National Guidance Committee, and the like[6]—none of these bodies ever represented all the Arabs of Israel.

Even more telling is the fact that the Arabs of Israel have not taken an active part in the *intifada*. The chief manifestations of this popular uprising in the occupied territories are extended commercial strikes, the disruption of public services (particularly the resignation of officials, policemen, and other employees of the civil administration), the crippling of the educational system, tax strikes, a boycott of Israeli goods, the murder of alleged collaborators, and daily violent demonstrations. None of these actions have taken place in Nazareth, Shefar'am, Umm al-Fahm, or other Arab settlements in Israel. There are of course occasional incidents of stone throwing, flying the Palestinian flag, and the painting of graffiti, but they are few and far between—they certainly do not add up to anything even resembling the *intifada*. One cannot compare what is happening on the streets in the occupied territories with life among the Arabs of Israel. Israeli journalists who visited the divided village of Bartaa, for example, were astonished by what they saw. Bartaa had been cut in two in 1948 by the border dividing Israel from the West Bank. It was ostensibly reunited in 1967, but the inhabitants of the village remained divided by their political status: half were Israeli citizens, the other half Jordanian citizens living under the rule of the Israeli military government. Since the outbreak of the *intifada* in December 1987, the people living in the eastern half of Bartaa have joined in the uprising by taking part in strikes and demonstrations, raising roadblocks, and so forth, while those on the Israeli side (like the rest of the Israeli-Arab community) have conspicuously refrained from doing so.

From time to time Israeli Arabs have taken the initiative in organizing shows of support for the Palestinians in the occupied territories—by means of rallies, fundraising events, strikes—as "a sign of solidarity," in the words of Dr. Azmi Bishara of Nazareth.[7] Yet solidarity is something one expresses in place of involvement. Nablus need not express its solidarity with Hebron because they are both engaged in the same struggle, but

Nazareth has felt the need to do so because it is following a different agenda. Even the PLO made it unequivocally clear to the Arabs of Israel that they were not expected to join in the uprising.[8]

As a rule, the Palestinians in the occupied territories and Arab states have come to understand and accept the fact that Israeli Arabs, though Palestinians themselves, live in a radically different political reality. The extent of this difference can be gauged from the results of the elections to Israel's twelfth Knesset in November 1988, which were held at the height of the *intifada*. Almost all the parties in Israel vied for the Arab vote, though there were actually only seven contenders: the Communist party,* the Progressive List for Peace, the Democratic Arab party (led by Abdul-Wahab Darawsha, who split with the Labor party to form his own list), the Labor party, *Mapam*, the Civil Rights and Peace Movement *(Ratz)*, and *Shinui* (the Center Movement). Three of the seven (the Communist party, the Progressive List for Peace, and the Democratic Arab party) are non-Zionist, even anti-Zionist, and derived almost all of their support from the Arab sector. A quick survey of the election propaganda indicates that the Progressive List for Peace focused on expressing its solidarity with the PLO and the Palestinian struggle in the occupied territories, whereas the Communist party and Darawsha divided their attention between the issue of equal rights for Israeli Arabs and the struggle for Palestinian independence. Had Israel's Arabs been interested in identifying primarily with the PLO, Palestinian nationalism, and the *intifada*, they would have voted in

---

* In its present incarnation as the Democratic Front for Peace and Equality, best known by its Hebrew acronym, *Hadash*.

large numbers for the Progressive List for Peace. In fact, they did not; the Progressive List received only one of the eleven seats ascribed to the votes of Israeli Arabs. The Communist party took four seats, and Darawsha one, while the remaining five mandates were distributed among three Zionist parties: *Ratz, Mapam,* and *Shinui.* In other words, even when the Palestinian struggle in the territories was at its height, over half of Israel's Arabs continued to place their own priorities first and therefore voted for the Zionist parties they believed would best promote their interests and advance their struggle for equal rights.

Salim Jubran, the editor of the Hadash newspaper *al-Itihad* ("Solidarity"), has commented that "a conflict of identities is superfluous. There is one solid, integral identity that sees peace (based upon two states for the two peoples) as both a Palestinian and an Israeli interest."[9] Thus in the political climate of the 1980s Jubran was able to regard himself as both an Israeli citizen concerned for the welfare of his country and a member of the Palestinian-Arab nation devoted to his people, whose blood, "spilled in the streets of the West Bank cities and villages," he wrote, "is my blood, the blood of my brothers."[10] The poet Hanna Abu-Hanna has similarly explained the ostensible paradox as follows: "It's true that I am a member of the Palestinian people. I shall be happy if the Palestinians achieve a homeland of their own. I will aid this homeland to the best of my ability, with financial contributions and perhaps with advice. But I have no intention of moving to [a Palestinian] state, when and if it is established. I am a citizen of Israel, and I will continue to live here."[11]

When the subjects of a number of research projects

investigating the status, rights, and identity of Israeli Arabs[12] were asked whether they would emigrate to a Palestinian state in the occupied territories, should such a state come into being, the overwhelming majority replied with a categorical no. In this they resembled Hanna Abu-Hanna and Tawfig Zayyad, who declared that not even a "cosmic upheaval" could force him to leave or renounce his attachment to his land. Many Israeli Arabs regard the very posing of such questions as a provocation; some even interpret it as a veiled threat to expel them from their homes and lands. An independent and prosperous Palestinian state encompassing Nablus, Hebron, and Gaza—and perhaps extending to East Jerusalem and even the East Bank of the Jordan— holds no lure for the Arab citizens of Israel. Even Palestinian nationalists living in the Israeli village of Baqa al-Gharbiya have no desire whatever to move two kilometers eastward to the West Bank village of Baqa al-Sharkiya, which would be part of the Palestinian state. The Israeli residents of the previously divided village of Bartaa would not even move 100 meters within their own village to a section that would fall within the boundaries of the sovereign state of Palestine.

The writer Anton Shammas has dismissed the question of whether or not he would move to a Palestinian state as having no bearing on his life. He contends that not only have Israeli Arabs never had any thought of leaving, the issue doesn't even exist for them. It is a problem for the Jews, not for the Palestinians. And so he dropped the issue back in Israel's lap. "The question is not where the Palestinians who are citizens of Israel will want to live on the day after a Palestinian state is declared," Shammas wrote, "but where the State of Israel wants them to live."[13]

Professor Joseph Ginat of Haifa University takes an optimistic view of the future development of the Israeli-Arab community. He believes that Israeli Arabs constitute a local-national identity whose elements are unique —a sort of "sub-identity" or "sub-branch" of the Palestinian-Arab entity whose boundaries are the same as the pre-1967 borders (the Green Line).[14] The main elements of this Israeli-Arab-Palestinian identity are: involvement in Israeli national life, a knowledge of Hebrew, and the struggle for equality. Among second-generation Israeli Arabs, there are indeed many professionals and public servants who have broken out of the confines of their ethnic community. They include novelists and journalists who write in Hebrew, actors in the Hebrew theater, and producers of Hebrew films. And although these figures are still relatively few in number, they are often in the forefront of Israel's cultural life.

Professor Sami Smouha of Haifa University is also of the opinion that a community whose culture is both Arab and Israeli has developed in the State of Israel, that it has a strong commitment to Israel's democratic system, regards itself as being on a civic par with the country's Jews, and sees its future in Israel. The Israeli Arab "is a proud, sensitive, self-respecting person who sees himself as a member of the Palestinian people . . . [and] advocates the solution to the Palestinian [problem] . . . through the establishment of a Palestinian state in the West Bank and Gaza, alongside the State of Israel. He sees this solution as necessary not for himself but for his Palestinian brothers, since he has already thrown in his lot with Israel."[15]

In a sense, this development is not entirely surprising. In the Middle East (as in other parts of the world, notably Africa) new "national identities" came into being as the result of political borders drawn arbitrarily, and sometimes quite fortuitously, by the colonial powers. The separate national frameworks created early in the twentieth century in Iraq, Jordan, Saudi Arabia, the Gulf states, Syria, and Lebanon were built on rather flimsy foundations. Indeed, the boundaries fixed between the Arab countries followed from power struggles between the colonial states, rather than indigenous national differences. To a large extent this was how the borders of Palestine under the British Mandate were established as well.[16] Within a short time however, strong political entities and even a kind of particularistic nationalism—be it Syrian, Lebanese, Jordanian, or Iraqi —evolved within these arbitrary borders, and despite various pressures it has survived to this day. Thus neither Pan-Arabism nor any other political movement or influence has altered these originally artificial frontiers. Syria, for example, took the extension of the borders of Lebanon by the French in 1922 to be an act of territorial theft. Yet even though the Syrian army controls most of Lebanon today, Damascus has not seen fit to annex any part of that country. Even the major pro-Syrian factions in Lebanon insist that their country's distinct political identity be preserved. Similarly, the Arab minority in the Khuzistan district of Iran remained aloof from the Iraqi army when it invaded their country in 1980, just as the Shiites in Iraq—who comprise 50 percent of that country's population—ignored Khomeini's exhortations to place religious devotion above national loyalty and remained faithful to the Baghdad government during Iraq's long war with Iran.

It may therefore be that the traditional components of "belonging," whose implications seemed so dramatic in the context of the "rituals of return," can play a significant role in helping Israeli Arabs integrate more fully into the country's national life. Yet this process could also develop along very different lines. Eli Rekhess of Tel Aviv University contends that the strengthening of social and cultural ties between Israeli Arabs and the Palestinians in the occupied territories has spawned shared political expectations. His approach emphasizes the danger in Israel's Arabs identifying with Palestinian nationalism (PLO)—which is in conflict with the State of Israel. On the other hand, Anton Shammas believes that the real danger stems from Israel's inability to be first and foremost the state of its own citizens, including its Arab citizens, rather than being the state of Jews the world over. To some extent, the PLO adopted an approach similar to that of the Jewish state. At the 1988 Palestinian National Council in Algiers, it proclaimed that Palestine is the state of the Palestinians "wherever they may be."[17] Some see this as an attempt to soften the original Palestinian demand for return to a specific village or house. In other words, every exiled Palestinian will now be able to consider the new Palestinian state as his home. The focus would no longer be on the specific house that was lost to him and his family.

Thus if a Palestinian state does come into being—or as Shammas has put it, rather more caustically, "when the quarrel with the neighbors across the road comes to an end"—it will be necessary to "convene a meeting of the tenants committee to deal with the fundamental question: 'If this is the national home of the Jewish people, what are you—the Palestinian Arabs we forgot to expel in 1948—doing here? Are you part of the family? Rent-paying tenants? Are you subletting? Are you registered landowners?' Only Allah knows."[18]

10

THE UNITY OF THE
TWO RIVERBANKS

B e it in the form of the predicament of refugees who
dreamed of returning to their homeland, or of na-
tives who felt like strangers in their own country,
the harsh fate of Palestinians after 1948 bypassed the
lives of about one third of the country's inhabitants.
Over 400,000 people living in the mountainous region,
from Jenin in the north to Hebron in the south, remained on their land and became the subjects of a fa-
miliar regime, that of the kingdom of Jordan. This
region, known in ancient Jewish sources as Judea and
Samaria and known during the age of Roman-Byzan-
tine dominion as Palestina Prima, was the heartland of
the Arab community of Palestine. According to the UN
partition plan, this was to have been the center of the
Arab state to be carved out of pre-1948 Palestine. But
the Palestinian leadership categorically rejected the no-
tion of partition, and in 1948 five Arab military forces
fought in this area (occasionally in competition with

each other) against the establishment of the State of Israel. They included local units of irregulars, which usually took their orders from the lieutenants of the *mufti* of Jerusalem, Haj Amin al-Husseini (the leading figure in the Palestinian nationalist leadership); the Egyptian army, which had come up from the south and controlled the Hebron district as far as the outskirts of Jerusalem; the Jordanian Arab Legion, commanded by British and Arab officers; an Iraqi expeditionary force that fought in Samaria; and a militia of volunteers, commanded by Fawzi al-Kaukji, that fought in northern Samaria at the beginning of the conflict. By the end of the war, only the Arab Legion remained in the area, and that fact was to determine its future political identity as an integral part of Transjordan.

The regime of Transjordan's King Abdullah could certainly not be characterized as "alien" to the Arabs of Palestine. A scion of the Hashemite family, whose ancestors had ruled in Mecca and Hijaz for centuries and traced their lineage to the Prophet Mohammed himself, Abdullah aspired to unify the whole of the Fertile Crescent under his dominion and viewed the annexation of the West Bank as the first step in this direction. Thus he had fostered connections with the Arabs of Palestine well before 1948. Over the previous two and a half decades, under the protection of the British, the king had created and established the administration of the Transjordan Emirate, in which he included notables from the West Bank. In fact, the creation of Transjordan's ruling bureaucracy and the development of its capital at Amman would probably have been impossible without the contribution of the Palestinians. Among those who were instrumental in shaping the character of the kingdom during its early years were Tawfiq Abu-Alhuda from Acre, who joined the royal administration in 1922 and served a number of terms as prime minister, and various members of the al-Rifa'i family (especially Samir, Abd al-Munim, and Ziyad). Although the mainstream Palestinian leadership did not support Abdullah's aspirations during the period of the British Mandate, the king was able to find allies among the opponents of Haj Amin al-Husseini, many of them members of large and wealthy families such as the Nashashibis, Khalidis, Dajanis, and Jarallahs of Jerusalem and the al-Jabri, al-Barghuti, Shawa, Farouki, al-Kheiri, Karzoun, al-Masri, and Hanun families from other parts of the country.

True to his aspirations, King Abdullah annexed the sector of Palestine occupied by his troops in December 1948 and four months later replaced the military administration there with a civil one. From then on the annexed area was called the "West Bank." Jordanian citizenship was granted to both the area's permanent residents and the refugees who had fled there during the fighting, and both elements were brought into the country's civil service. In May 1949 notables from the West Bank were appointed as ministers in the Jordanian government. In April 1950 the new citizens of Jordan on the West Bank participated in the elections to Parliament, which officially proclaimed the annexation of the West Bank. The country's name, moreover, was changed to the Hashemite Kingdom of Jordan.

Many members of the families that had cooperated with Abdullah during the days of the British Mandate now helped him to extend his rule to the West Bank as ministers, members of Parliament, and senior officials.

Once the king's administration was firmly established in the West Bank, a number of his opponents reversed their position and chose to back the new regime. Anwar Nusseibeh from East Jerusalem, for example, who had been a follower of Haj Amin al-Husseini and served as the secretary of the symbolic government Husseini formed in Gaza in 1948, returned to Jerusalem in 1949 and went to work for the Jordanian administration, eventually rising to senior positions. Moreover, refugees who had fled to the West Bank, and a few of those who had crossed the river and settled on the eastern side, were also appointed to government posts. The refugees were enfranchised, just like the indigenous residents of these areas, and some were even appointed as ministers or elected to Parliament—half of whose members were required, by law, to come from the West Bank.

The situation of the refugees on both banks of the Hashemite kingdom was far more agreeable than that of their counterparts in Lebanon and Gaza. With the exception of the people living in the cluster of camps near Jericho, the refugees on the West Bank were dispersed among twenty small and usually isolated camps, a number of which eventually took on the character of small and poor rural neighborhoods. Other refugees were dispersed in small groups on the outskirts of hundreds of West Bank villages and towns.

From the very outset the Jordanian regime took pains to ensure that the kingdom's center of gravity would be on the East Bank, whose sparse (450,000) and mostly poor population in 1948 was composed largely of Bedouin tribesmen (the rest being residents of small towns and Circassian and Muslim Chechen immigrants who had been resettled in eastern Jordan during the waning days of the Ottoman Empire). The deliberate cultivation of the East Bank and its capital at Amman was also designed as a way of averting the growth of bases of social, economic, and particularly political power in the West Bank. The court was keenly aware that while it was working to develop the kingdom's national identity under the slogan "the unity of the two banks," such power bases could well become hotbeds of Palestinian nationalism and separatist demands.

As part of the program favoring the East Bank, the area was granted substantial economic benefits, and it was chosen as the location for government offices, public institutions, industrial and development projects, and a network of medical, educational, and cultural institutions. The West Bank, in contrast, was sorely neglected, and East Jerusalem's special status was played down. The teacher and journalist Muhammad Abu-Shilbaya, a refugee who had settled in East Jerusalem, wrote many years after the fact about the Jordanians' arrogance in broadcasting the Friday prayers live from the central mosque in Amman, which has no special standing in the Arab world, rather than from the al-Aqsa Mosque in Jerusalem, the third most important Islamic site (after Mecca and Medina). "If the Jordanians had been able to do so, they would have transferred Jerusalem's Old City walls to Amman," he wrote angrily.[1] Jerusalem's administrative status was inferior to that of Amman, and its municipal boundaries were intentionally constricted.[2] The Hashemite royal family did not even maintain an official residence in Jerusalem, and it wasn't until shortly before the Six-Day War that the construction of a royal palace began in Beit Hanina, north of the city.

As a result of this policy, from 1948 onward there was a major wave of migration over the river from the West Bank. It embraced both refugees and members of the indigenous population, urban as well as rural dwellers, and people from all classes and walks of life (including Christian Arabs from Jerusalem, Ramallah, and Bethlehem). Between 1948 and 1967 an estimated half million people moved to the East Bank, and many continued onward to the oil-producing states in the Persian Gulf, where they found employment but were denied citizenship. These *"Gastarbeiter"* sent their savings back to their families on both banks. Thus emigration and the job opportunities available in the Gulf states eased the pressures so characteristic of refugee life in Gaza and Lebanon but also helped to obscure the special identity of the refugees.

The Jordanian establishment tried to suppress all signs of solidarity and cooperation between the Arabs of the West Bank (or the East Bank who had come from Palestine) and the Palestinian refugees in Gaza, Lebanon, and elsewhere. Any attempt to create a distinctly Palestinian political framework was viewed as a potential threat to the new "Jordanian identity" developing on the two banks. Hardly any institutions, public or commercial companies, or cultural organizations in Jordan had the word "Palestine" in their name; nor were any streets or squares graced with that appellation. The country's domestic and foreign policy strove to foster assimilation by denying the Palestinians' distinct identity and converting them into Jordanians. This approach was not only contrary to the desire of many of the Palestinians in Jordan, but it also flew in the face of the consensus in almost the entire Arab world.

Thus it should not be surprising that the Jordanian

regime's attempts to assimilate the Palestinians into the new "Jordanian entity" met with opposition from Palestinian quarters as far back as 1948. Some of these opposition forces received support from the other Arab states, which viewed Jordan's annexation of the West Bank with great suspicion, as they did Abdullah's designs on the whole of the Fertile Crescent. In July 1951, however, a Palestinian assassinated King Abdullah at the entrance to the al-Aqsa Mosque. (Among the plotters who were tried and executed for the murder was a member of the Husseini family.) In the ensuing years Palestinians continued to head the groups that opposed the Jordanian regime, including the *Ba'ath* and Communist parties, the National Socialist party, and fanatical Muslim movements. Thus while the Jordanian regime embraced the Palestinians and was generous in bestowing benefits on its loyalists, it remained fundamentally suspicious of the refugees and of the West Bankers as a whole—an attitude that never really changed. Very few Palestinians were appointed to sensitive posts in the army or the internal-security apparatus, just as there were few Palestinians to be found among the king's close associates or the regime's leading decision makers.

The evolution of a distinct Palestinian consciousness at the end of the 1950s and beginning of the 1960s was therefore a challenge to the official Jordanian ideology. In 1964, when the PLO was established by a resolution of the second Arab summit conference in Alexandria, this new outlook received an organizational expression, and the Arab world forced Jordan to accept the new political framework. Hence with profound misgivings and considerable dissatisfaction, King Hussein agreed to permit the founding assembly of the PLO in East

Jerusalem.[3] However, a year and a half later, in July 1966, the Jordanian government closed the PLO's offices, claiming that the head of the organization, Ahmed Shukeiri, was engaged in "Communist activities." It was a rather lame excuse, for everyone knew that the crux of the problem was that the Jordanian authorities could not accept an organization that implied a separate Palestinian existence, since that would necessarily undermine the annexation of the West Bank and create for Jordan's Palestinian citizens an object of political and national allegiance that clashed with their loyalty to Amman.

Despite these problems, Jordan succeeded in preserving the integrity of the Hashemite kingdom, essentially because its policy did not pose a threat to the traditional element of the West Banker's identity: their strong attachment to their homes and land. Palestinians moved to the East Bank in order to find work, open businesses, or take up public and government positions in Amman, which was just a two-hour drive from Nablus, Ramallah, or Hebron. Almost every West Bank family, including the refugees, had a "branch" in Amman, which gradually grew into a large Palestinian city. But their traditional traits of attachment to the village, neighborhood, house, and extended family in the West Bank remained as strong as ever. Moreover, the Hashemite regime wisely cultivated and embraced the pillars of traditional Palestinian social structure: the heads of old and wealthy families, landowners, sheikhs and *mukhtars*, the rural community (with its residual tribal character), and the conservative religious establishment. And it was such policies that enabled the regime to weather political storms until the Six-Day War broke out and changed the picture entirely.

11

STATE LANDS

The 1967 war created yet another wave of refugees: an estimated 300,000 inhabitants of the West Bank and Gaza who fled to the East Bank of the Jordan. Most of them were "veterans" fleeing for the second time. This category included many residents of the large refugee camps around Jericho and in Gaza who, for the first time in twenty years, were able to make the short journey across Israel and the West Bank into the Jordanian heartland. They did not leave land or permanent dwellings behind them; they merely continued their wanderings. They were joined, however, by thousands of new refugees, most of them fleeing out of fear of the Israelis. Others, such as the inhabitants of a number of villages destroyed in the fighting along the border between Israel and the West Bank (the Green Line), were forcibly expelled by the army. A number of villagers in this category—notably the residents of a few streets in Kalkilya and of Beit Mirsim in the Hebron hills—returned after the war to rebuild their homes with the permission of the Israeli authorities. But they were the exception to the rule. Denied the right to return, the inhabitants of Imwas, Beit Noba, and Yalu—three villages in the Latrun areas that were totally devastated— joined the ranks of the refugees.

Still, the overwhelming majority of the residents of the West Bank and Gaza Strip, including the 1948 refugees, stayed put in 1967. These included almost all of the local leadership, former Jordanian cabinet members, senators, members of parliament, mayors, and people in key positions in the Jordanian establishment. Why didn't they flee, as an earlier generation had in 1948? Perhaps because the war was over so quickly that they barely had a chance to react. In 1967 the West Bank was conquered in a mere four days, while in 1948 the fighting had extended over months, edging through village after village, street after street. Or perhaps the explanation lies in the words of Sheikh Muhammad Ali al-Ja'abari, then mayor of Hebron, who told Moshe Dayan that the Arabs had learned from the experience of the 1948 refugees that it was better to die than become homeless seminomads.[1] Ja'abari claimed that the king of Saudi Arabia promised to set him up in a palace if he were to flee, but he had declined the offer. "Better to die in my own poor house than to live in a palace in Arabia," he told journalists who asked him whether he was fearful of the Jews exacting revenge.[2]

Thus the inhabitants of the West Bank did not, for the most part, become refugees in 1967. But they slowly began to face a new danger: that their traditional identity would be weakened by the rule of the non-Arab authority that had replaced the Arab regime in which they had been partners. The special implications of Israel's rule over the occupied territories began to make themselves felt almost immediately after the fighting ended. East Jerusalem was annexed to the State of Israel but its residents were not granted Israeli citizenship. As permanent residents of the city, these Palestinians came under the jurisdiction of Israeli law and were eligible for national health benefits and social security. They could also participate in municipal elections (as could the foreign consuls and other diplomats residing in the city), but, lacking citizenship, they were not entitled to vote in Israeli national elections for the Knesset. The rest of the people of the West Bank remained under a military government that curtailed their freedom and civil rights considerably and, obviously, denied them citizenship.

Israel's policy toward the Arabs in the West Bank and East Jerusalem was radically different from the approach adopted two decades earlier toward the Arabs living in Israel proper (upon whom Israeli citizenship had been imposed). Mahmoud al-Khatib, a journalist who published a daily column in the East Jerusalem newspaper *a-Sh'ab*,[3] compared the new status of the Palestinians in the occupied West Bank and Gaza Strip to the changing models of an automobile. The Israeli Arabs of Nazareth, Shefar'am, and Umm al-Fahm were "1948-model Arabs," and those in the West Bank and Gaza were "1967-model Arabs." But while the two "models" exhibited distinct differences—due to the nineteen years of Israeli rule, as well as various legal and political arrangements—they still had much in common.

It was no accident, therefore, that following 1967, and especially at the beginning of the 1970s, the Arab world as a whole and the Palestinian organizations in particular began to display a heightened interest in the Arabs of Israel. Israel's domination of the large Palestinian population in the West Bank and Gaza inevitably drew attention to the community of Palestinians who had already been subject to Israeli rule for over two decades. In the 1950s and 1960s the Arab world had taken little interest in them, dismissing this unique branch of the Palestinian community as "the Arab minority in conquered Palestine," "the Palestinians in the conquered territory," or "the Arabs from the conquered part of the stolen homeland." But when the conquest of the West Bank and Gaza extended Israeli rule over more than a million additional Palestinians, the Arabs of Israel ceased to be exceptional, and this was precisely what generated such great interest in them. Their brothers were now eager to learn how they had survived under the Israeli yoke while honoring the principle of *summud* (resolution to cling to the soil of the homeland).

In 1966, shortly before the Six-Day War, Ghassan Kanafani published excerpts from his book *Resistance Literature in Conquered Palestine* in the Lebanese monthly *al-Aadab*. It was the first time that considerable attention was paid to works by Arabs who were subject to Israeli rule. Until then the term "Palestinian literature" had referred to the corpus of works by writers who had been exiled from Palestine or lived in the West Bank and Gaza, never to Israeli Arabs.[4] Kanafani was apparently the first to discover the writings of Mahmoud Darwish, Samih al-Qasim, Tawfiq Zayyad, Emil Habibi, and Salim Jubran and to dub them the creators of the "resistance literature." Following the Six-Day War these writers became heroes in the Arab world. Their works

were published in many editions (mainly in Beirut),
quoted on the radio and at public meetings, and they
were showered with praise. The Syrian poet Nizar Qabbani, among the most famous writers in the Arab
world, immortalized them in 1968 in writing "To the
Poets of the Conquered Land":

> *We have been learning from you for many years now,*
> *We defeated poets,*
> *We to whom history and grief are strangers,*
> *We have learned from you that a letter is shaped like a knife!*
>
> *
>
> *Oh you who sharpen your pencils on your ribs,*
> *We are learning from you how to explode mines with words,*
> *Poets of the occupied land . . .*
> *Standing beside your poems,*
> *Our bards look like dwarfs.*[5]

Why this sudden outpouring of admiration for the
hitherto provincial and unrecognized "resistance literature" created by Galilean villagers and members of the
Haifa editorial board of *al-Itihad*, all writers working
under Israeli rule? The scholar Gideon Shiloh believes
that it stemmed from the wave of guilt and self-
reproach that swept through the Arab world after the
terrible defeat of 1967.[6] During this period the spokesmen of the "resistance" among Israeli Arabs were a
kind of anchor or foil for the rest of the Arabs. Until
1967 the Arab world, and Arab literature as its reflection, had wallowed in self-indulgence, decadence, and
corruption, "riding on rocking horses and battling
ghosts and phantoms," in the words of Nizar Qabbani.
And how better to measure the degree of decadence
than by juxtaposing it with the power and the glory of
the "resistance," the proud and brave endurance of the

Arabs of Israel, who were compared to "a rosebush growing out of embers," to "blessed rain that falls despite oppression and compulsion," to "the song of a drowning man from the depths of a well," to "a buried man rising to his feet."

There was considerable importance to the cultural and political climate prevailing among the Arabs in the occupied territories after 1967, because they adopted the "resistance" of the Arabs of the Galilee, Haifa, and the Triangle as the mold in which to cast their own experience of *summud*. This process was aided by a number of Israeli Arabs who left the country to join the ranks of the PLO, the most prominent among them being Mahmoud Darwish, Sabri Jiryis, Habib Qahawaji, Imad Shaqur, and Elias Shoufani. Their own experience made them quickly realize the fact that masses of Palestinians in the West Bank and Gaza who were now under Israeli rule created a new reality. Since the occupation had not displaced them from their homeland, the inhabitants of the occupied territories had joined the cycle of Palestinian suffering not due to their longing to return to their homes and lands but because of their determination not to leave them—because of *summud*.

Paradoxically, though perhaps predictably, Israel's policy in the occupied territories induced the Palestinians to seek their identity through a new "Palestinian entity," in the form of the PLO, rather than in a Jordanian or other framework. They believed that Israel wanted to uproot them and turn them into refugees or strangers in their own land, for this had become the national condition of the Palestinians after 1948. And the fact is that there are several illustrations that bear this contention out. The Israeli military government issued regulations restricting the mobility of the population in order to minimize the number of people entitled to the status of permanent residents in the territories. Hundreds of thousands of inhabitants of the West Bank, Gaza, and East Jerusalem who traveled to the East Bank or other Arab countries to visit, to work, or to study for extended periods discovered that they could not return to their homes in the territories. At the end of 1967 the military government conducted a census and issued identity cards certifying their bearers as permanent residents of the territories only to those people who were present on the day of the count.[7] Other people who may have been abroad at the time but wished to reside in the West Bank and Gaza had to submit a special request to be reunified with their families. Israel announced that the following categories of people would have their requests approved: a husband wishing to return to his wife in the territories (or a wife to her husband); parents wishing to repatriate a son or daughter aged sixteen or under; orphaned grandchildren aged sixteen or under; parents over the age of sixty who wished to be with their children; and other cases of a special humanitarian nature.[8] Clearly the policy was to prevent the return of males between the ages of sixteen and sixty, primarily for security reasons but also in an attempt to limit the birth rate in the territories. Up to 1972 Israel allowed about 45,000 people to return to the territories and be reunited with their families—a small minority of those who had applied. According to an officer in the military government,[9] hundreds of thousands of Palestinians who appealed for permission to return during the civil war in Jordan (September 1970 to

July 1971) were turned down. Israel subsequently allowed a maximum of 1,000 people a year to return under the rubric of the "reunification of families." But since most of the petitions were rejected (at the beginning of the 1980s the number of refused petitions stood at approximately 150,000), the Palestinians gradually ceased applying. Other restrictions were imposed upon inhabitants of the territories who went abroad, and if they failed to fulfill the conditions necessary for renewing their residence papers, they too lost the right to return.

Even when applications to return permanently to the occupied territories were rejected, almost all the Palestinians who so requested were allowed to visit. Entry visas were valid for one to three months and could be extended. Especially during the school vacations, usually in the summer months, the territories were virtually inundated with visitors, whose number reached into the hundreds of thousands. The military government proudly publicized the fact that masses of Arabs from neighboring countries were able to visit and tour the territories. But as Dr. Walid Qamhawi, a physician from Nablus, pointedly remarked to journalists, "These people are neither visitors from Arab countries nor tourists coming for a summer visit. They are Palestinians who work in foreign countries, and their only home is in the territories." [10]

The Jordan River was now the new border. Israeli restrictions on movement across this border created a barrier between the hundreds of thousands of Palestinians who lived outside the territories, and their families and land in the West Bank and Gaza. A new threat loomed—the two groups of Palestinians might be severed one from the other. Family members were now termed "summer visitors" by the authorities; they were only "tourists" who had no right to their own homeland.

Even more troubling for the Arabs in the occupied territories was concern over the fate of their property, given the Israeli policy on land, water, and construction. The Israelis resorted to a variety of methods to expropriate land or restrict its use by Arabs. Real estate and assets registered in the names of nonresidents ("absentee owners") were declared "abandoned" and transferred to Israeli custody. In a sweeping operation that began in 1980, the military government defined "state lands" as large tracts of mostly rock-strewn land to which the local Arabs could not conclusively prove ownership. Other land was expropriated for public use, declared a "closed area for military purposes," or requisitioned for military use as "combat areas" or "firing zones." Major construction was prohibited on land adjacent to main roads, military installations, and Jewish settlements. Broad areas were declared "nature sanctuaries," and various restrictions were placed on the cultivation of land by Arabs. By the end of the 1980s it was estimated that over half the area of the West Bank had been removed from Arab control and placed in Israeli hands.[11]

The 1970s and 1980s were years of economic prosperity in the territories. Large sums flowed in from family members working in Israel and the Gulf states, enabling the inhabitants to invest in education and the construction of private housing. One result was a building boom in the territories that began in 1974 and peaked in 1981.[12] This huge increase in private building was also fueled by capital from the Arab states and the PLO (known as *summud* funds). Eventually the building activity in the territories, like control over the land, became the object of a fierce political struggle. The price of land skyrocketed, and though construction opportunities remained almost unlimited in Arab towns, the Israelis restricted building in the villages, where 65 percent of the population resides and where it has come virtually to a halt since the mid-1980s.

These facts serve to explain the frustration and anxiety that beset the Palestinians at that time. With the onset of a recession in the oil-producing states, the flow of money into the territories declined appreciably. At the same time, thousands of high school and college graduates who would otherwise have sought jobs in the Persian Gulf remained in the West Bank and Gaza. Educated but lacking suitable job prospects, they had little choice but to engage in manual labor, mostly in the building trades and cleaning services in Israel. In the winter of 1986, when an Israeli journalist phoned a lecturer at Bir-Zeit University from an office building in Tel Aviv, he noticed that a young Arab cleaning worker was eavesdropping on the conversation. When the journalist[13] later asked the young man if he was acquainted with the teacher from Bir-Zeit, he replied "Yes, I completed my M.A. with him last year."

Asked what it was that bothered him most about Israeli rule, Rashad a-Shawa, a onetime mayor of Gaza and among the wealthier figures in the territories, replied: "The feeling that my grandson and his children may be destined to wash dishes in the restaurants on Dizengoff Street" (in Tel Aviv).

The employment of Palestinians in Israel, and to a

certain extent in the Arab oil states, stepped up the proletarianization of what had largely been an agrarian society in the territories. The trend toward steering Palestinians into unskilled jobs within Israel was perceived as another calculated attempt to destroy their ties to the soil of their homeland. As early as 1975 an East Jerusalem theater group chose to perform an adaptation of a famous tale about an old farmer who tells his sons that a great treasure is hidden on their land. Rushing out to the field, the sons plough up every square foot of it but find nothing. Then they realize that the diligent working of the land is the true treasure. The message to the Palestinians was clear.

Vigorous Israeli settlement activity further heightened the Palestinians' fear of dispossession. When the Labor government fell in May 1977, there were about 5,000 settlers in the thirty-four Jewish settlements on the West Bank (twenty-one of which were in the Jordan Valley and six more in the Etzion Bloc north of Hebron). Some fifteen years later, at the beginning of the 1990s, the number of Jewish settlements in the West Bank and Gaza Strip exceeded 130 with a population of about 100,000 people. Despite warnings from Washington, in the summer of 1991 the Israeli government went into particularly high gear in expanding the number of housing projects in the territories.

Jewish settlement after the Six-Day War passed through a number of phases. At first it was carried out by a small number of zealous nationalists, the majority of them observant Jews, who founded a movement called *Gush Emmunim* to reestablish Jewish sovereignty in Judea and Samaria, the most historically significant parts of the Holy Land. Successive Labor governments approved the building of settlements only for security purposes and limited them to the sparsely populated Jordan Valley. After the 1973 war, however, under pressure from *Gush Emmunim*, even Labor agreed to a certain degree of settlement in areas heavily populated by Palestinians, thus setting a precedent for the policy advanced by the Likud government after 1977. The Likud never concealed its aim of extending Jewish sovereignty to all of the historic land of Israel. Settlement in the occupied territories was therefore a prime test of its resolve, and it readily offered economic incentives to draw Israelis over the Green Line.

The main increase in Jewish population dated to the period between 1980 and 1986, the same years in which there was a decline in Arab construction due to the recession in the oil-producing states and a drastic cutback in the number of permits issued for building in the villages. Before issuing such permits, the military government's Planning and Building Authority demanded definitive proof of land ownership, the submission of master plans, and the preparation of the infrastructure, including access roads, sanitary installations, and facilities for garbage disposal. Jewish settlements in the territories were built almost exclusively by public bodies—such as the Ministry of Housing, the Jewish Agency, and construction companies owned by the settlement movements—which were equipped to fulfill these standard Israeli requirements. But the Arabs building individually for their personal needs had difficulty meeting them. The Israelis essentially required them to change their traditional way of life, to crowd together in housing developments, and even to construct multistory buildings if they wanted to enjoy the array of services that typify a modern way of life. An Arab engineer from Tulkarem described the situation this way: "When a Jew lives in a small apartment on the third floor in a crowded neighborhood in the outskirts of Tel Aviv, he is told to go live in a beautiful place in the West Bank, where he'll have a house with a large garden. That's what 'quality of life' means. But if an Arab wants to build a beautiful house with a garden on the outskirts of his village, he's told to go live on the third floor in the middle of the village—that's 'quality of life' for him."

In October 1988 Dr. Sari Nusseibeh wrote that the existence of the Palestinian people in the territories depended upon two basic elements, land and water, and that Israel had seized control of both.[14] Though the Palestinians still exercised a certain hold over their land, Israel had assumed full control over the water, since the West Bank is the source of one quarter of Israel's limited reserves of this crucial resource. The Israelis, moreover, practiced discrimination in allocating water in the territories. At the end of the 1980s, the 70,000 Jews living in the West Bank and Gaza accounted for 40 percent of the water consumption, while the remaining 60 percent of the water was distributed among the territories' one and a half million Arabs. Seen in other terms, thirty or so Jewish settlements in the territories were allotted approximately the same amount of water as 450 Arab settlements.[15] But the statistics on water are only one aspect of what the Palestinians call the "economic siege"; it is also expressed in the failure to develop an infrastructure in the territories, the prohibition on founding industries that might compete with Israeli concerns, and a discriminatory tax policy.

The Israeli authorities seem to have discovered the

Palestinians' most sensitive nerve in their struggle to hold on to their land and homes, for the two harshest punishments meted out to the Arabs in the territories are deportation and the demolition of houses. Other measures taken in a similar vein are the uprooting of trees (usually along the roadsides) that have provided cover for Arabs throwing stones or firebombs and a resolute policy of tearing down houses that have been built without permits. The Palestinians' dread of such punishments was well portrayed in a story written in 1976 by Akram Haniyeh, "That Village . . . That Morning." It is the tale of a dead man who rises from his grave to the sound of bulldozers clearing the land for a Jewish settlement only to discover that his house has disappeared, his son is in jail, and he himself has been sentenced to deportation. "Apart from Abu-Mahmud's groans, the cemetery was silent as usual. The military commander thought: If we arrest him there will be a problem: how can we arrest a man who has risen from the grave? . . . And the bulldozers are about to level the cemetery, so there won't be anywhere to return him to. . . . What shall we do with him? One of his adjutants, seeing the commander's predicament, walks over to him and whispers: 'We'll deport him to Jordan.' "[16] Akram Haniyeh was himself deported in 1986.

The Israeli regime in the territories thus revealed to be not just the rule of occupiers governing by virtue of a military presence and meting out punishments to protect the security of their own country but also a regime whose ultimate objective was to wear down the Palestinians and sever their bonds to their land. Dr. Sari Nusseibeh listed the features of Israel's policy devoted to this end as the expropriation of land and reduction of the water supply, bans on travel and construction, the "economic siege" and restrictions on the development of an independent Palestinian economy, the transformation of peasants into urban laborers (leading to the depopulation of rural areas), collective punishment, deportation, and the demolition of houses.[17] The Palestinians thus view Israel's policy in the territories as a tool for achieving its declared political aims. At the end of December 1977, Prime Minister Menachem Begin proposed a plan for Palestinian autonomy as a permanent solution to the competing political claims on the West Bank and Gaza Strip (a plan that was later incorporated in the Camp David agreements). The crux of Begin's program was that Israel would continue to maintain a military and civilian presence in the territories, control state lands, and supervise the distribution of water. The Begin government further stressed that autonomy was to be granted on a personal and communal basis, not a geographic one, meaning autonomy for the inhabitants rather than the territory—as though the people in question were totally divorced from the land upon which they live.

The growing power of the Likud party, coupled with the rise of political movements even further to the right, movements that advocate the "transfer" or deportation of the Arabs, had a resounding impact on the Palestinian mood. During the Israeli invasion of Lebanon—an operation aimed against Palestinians, not against the Lebanese—rumors abounded that Israel intended to drive the PLO and its Palestinian supporters out of not only southern Lebanon but also the country as a whole. Hints were liberally dropped in the occupied territories that under certain conditions—the outbreak of a regional conflict, for example—the plans to rid Lebanon of its Palestinian population would also be applied in the West Bank, Gaza Strip, and East Jerusalem. Repeated declarations by Israeli politicians (particularly by Ariel Sharon) that a Palestinian state already existed, in Jordan, left little doubt in the minds of the Palestinians that what the Israelis called "creeping annexation" was actually a deliberate effort to force them out of their homeland.

Israel's policy succeeded in clearly transmitting these messages to the Palestinians in the territories, and such signals are what finally sparked the *intifada,* or popular uprising, at the end of 1987. The "local identities" of the villagers in the Hebron hills, the remaining members of the Christian elite in Bethlehem, Jerusalem, and Ramallah, the merchants of Nablus, and the Bedouin in the Judean Desert were melded in the crucible of Israeli rule. True, these people were not reduced to the status of refugees, yet they were bound together by a more abstract, national allegiance based on their common struggle. Before 1967 the strong attachment to the clan, tribe, sect, village, or region had been a divisive factor in Palestinian society. But after the Six-Day War, Israel's menacing policy worked to weaken these loyalties. The sons of the glass blowers of Hebron and the soap merchants of Nablus, farmers and refugees, Christians and Muslims, Bedouin and townsfolk all found themselves working side by side on construction sites and flooding the job market in Israel's services, crafts, and industry. For the 1948 refugees it was the desire to return that bridged the gap between traditional loyalties; for the inhabitants of the territories conquered in 1967, it was Israeli rule that created a new type of solidarity—not the striving for a nostalgic, emotional return to past precincts but a shared aspiration to future independence.

12

BUT I
SHALL NOT RETURN

At the beginning of the 1990s the Palestinian population within the borders of what had been Palestine under the British Mandate numbered 2.3
million people, 1.6 million of whom were residents of
the Gaza Strip and the West Bank (including East Jerusalem). After 1967, it was this segment of the population that gradually became the center of the Israeli-Arab
conflict. While the fighting in 1948, 1956, and 1973 had
essentially been a clash between sovereign states, that
condition changed at the end of the 1970s with the signing of the peace treaty between Israel and Egypt, the
largest and most powerful of the Arab countries.
Egypt's departure from the ranks of the belligerents not
only eliminated the danger to Israel's southern frontier
but also lessened the probability of a concerted attack
by the other bordering states. At about the same time,
Iran and Iraq began their long and grueling war, tem-
porarily neutralizing the threat on Israel's eastern front.

The focus of the Middle East conflict thus turned away from Israel's borders to the country's interior—the occupied territories. Needless to say, the Arab states did not desert the arena altogether. "The Arab countries never ceased to view Israel as irksome and dangerous," Professor Bernard Lewis noted in a conversation at Teddy Kollek's house in the summer of 1989, "but they discovered that they had many other problems that were more irksome and more dangerous." The unrelenting tension between Jerusalem and Cairo, as well as between Jerusalem and Amman, Damascus and Baghdad, had spawned similar tension between Jerusalem and Jerusalem—between the Israeli Jews and Palestinian Arabs living in the same country and the same capital. The crux of the conflict had shifted, or perhaps returned, to Palestine's Arabs, half of whom were subject to Israeli rule and half scattered east of the Jordan (refugees or émigrés who mostly held Jordanian citizenship) or in Lebanon, Syria, and the Gulf states (where they were denied citizenship). This change in focus found its most dramatic expression in the uprising that erupted at the end of 1987 and redefined the essence of the Palestinian experience as "nation building,"[1] the social processes by which past traditions merge with modern Western values to create the new format of a people and a state.

In the political climate of the late 1970s and early 1980s, the prime demand made by the Palestinians and the Arab states was the termination of Israeli rule in the West Bank and Gaza Strip, which was regarded as a "colonial situation."[2] The justification for this demand was the Palestinians' claim to the right of national self-determination. That required them first to prove the existence of a Palestinian nation, which many quarters were working to deny. Thus if, for the previous two decades, the refugees had been obsessively engaged in yearning to return, they were now equally preoccupied with developing a distinctly Palestinian national identity. The decline of the Pan-Arab dream of unification and the pronounced divisiveness within the Arab world at the time created convenient conditions for tackling this task.

"Until 1967," the critic Jamil Shalhout observed, "local scholars showed only a limited interest in the popular Palestinian heritage."[3] In fact, few literary or scientific works were published on this subject throughout British rule, the most prominent of them being Dr. Tawfiq Kana'an's research on the traditions of popular medicine, the legends surrounding the sacred burial sites, and popular sayings, and Aref al-Aref's book on the Bedouin in the Beersheba district. The next two decades saw the publication of studies on Palestinian literature and an encyclopedia of Palestinian folklore by Nimr Sirhan. But the 1980s witnessed a virtual flood of publications and an upsurge in Palestinian cultural activity in every sphere. Universities and research institutes, museums and theaters, archives and publishing houses in the territories and beyond devoted themselves to a wide range of subjects, from Palestinian dress, embroidery, weaving, dyeing, and ornamentation,[4] to traditional craft tools, agricultural methods, and rural construction.[5] Scores of popular dance and song troupes were founded.[6] Studies were published on Palestinian humor,[7] customs, tales of ghosts and demons,[8] the theme of the land in Palestinian stories, labor songs,[9] desert songs,[10] children's and fishermen's songs,[11] traditional musical instruments, the traditional educational system, the significance of the olive tree, labor relations and the class structure,[12] the structure of the clan, popular tales and proverbs, economics, literature, theater, and poetry.[13] Archives and documentation centers were opened.[14] Ancient maps were collected. The works of Palestinian artists were shown locally and abroad. Tours were arranged for song, dance, and theatrical troupes. Countless conferences were organized (usually around the theme of "Palestine Week") where findings on the uniqueness of the Palestinian heritage were reported. Palestinian myths and heroic stories were reconstructed, some embellished, others fabricated.

All of these activities were designed to grant legitimacy to the idea that there is a Palestinian people, a people that may not have existed before but one that had acquired an identity through the cultivation of its heritage. In this fostering or even fabricating of a heritage, one can definitely see an effort to "convert" (as the historian Emanuel Sivan put it) "a plain territorial state (which is often solely the result of a colonial partition) into a 'community with a collective memory,' that is, a nation-state."[15] Admittedly, where the Palestinians are concerned one cannot speak of a territorial state, for they never had one. But they do dwell in areas (the territories) where they must defend themselves against the Israeli threat to their national character.

The concept of *summud*, of "sticking to the homeland," fitted in well with the cultivation of a national heritage as a mechanism of struggle and defense. Since 1967 it has been clear to the Palestinians living in the territories that the greatest danger to their collective being lies in compromising on their attachment to their heritage and their land. Soon after the Six-Day War, when Israel began to expropriate land in East Jerusalem, the Arab owners refused to accept the financial compensation offered by the government, since the taking of money was regarded as a sign of being resigned to the loss of both the land and the heritage that went along with it. The sale of property to Israelis was equated with treason. Real estate agents who dared to handle such transactions, through various ruses, were branded as the most despicable of collaborators. Arab employment in all branches of the Israeli economy, including the construction of Jewish settlements in the territories, may have been countenanced as a necessary evil; but selling land was like selling one's national legacy and, with it, the hope of an emergent Palestinian nationalism.

The upsurge in private Arab construction in the territories during the past two decades was prompted by more than a desire to improve the Palestinians' quality of life and strengthen their ties to the land; it was an expression of hope. A man who invests all his savings in building a new house expresses his faith in the future. The building is designed as a home for his children and grandchildren, for future generations of the extended family. Yet even when land was being expropriated on every side and the Israelis were building settlements on it, thus jeopardizing the Arab presence in the territories, the Palestinians remained undaunted. Under similar circumstances other people might have chosen to invest in savings or readily liquidated assets, such as gold, diamonds, and foreign currency, to avoid losing everything should they find themselves forced into exile. But the Palestinians living in the territories have invested in a wide range of private construction. They have built in the cities and the villages. Even thousands of the 1948 refugees who managed to extricate themselves from camps and rented apartments in slums have sunk all their assets into regaining a foothold on the land.

The momentum of construction in the territories was also a reflection of the steep rise in the standard of living during the first years of the occupation.[16] At the same time, modern social trends began to have an impact upon the traditional social structure—a process that was accelerated by the extended isolation from the East Bank. In the 1950s the monarchal regime in Jordan, which by its nature is traditional and semifeudal, integrated the West Bank by embracing the leading members of the old social system. The heads of the large and distinguished families were appointed as ministers, senators, and members of Parliament, and the prestige of the older generation of notables—the sheiks, effendis, beys, *mukhtars,* who were the major landowners—remained intact. Nevertheless, from 1967 onwards their power steadily waned, so that by the time of the *intifada* their very presence was hardly felt.

Under Jordanian rule, these traditional leaders were able to lavish upon their constituents the spoils of power—such as government jobs, loans, and licenses—and they were also the major suppliers of employment, so that the livelihoods of both the peasants and the refugees depended on the major landowners and industrialists. After 1967, however, the Israeli labor market opened up to the inhabitants of the territories. No longer did they have to turn to the old aristocracy for work. Work in Israel was more convenient, better paying, and offered a small portion of Israeli workman's benefits, which are superior to those granted by Arab employers.

On top of this change, the traditional elite in the territories lost a number of its exclusive status symbols. Whereas in the past only the wealthy and distinguished families could afford to send their children to universities in the Arab countries or overseas, the prosperity of the 1970s and the opening of colleges and universities in the territories enabled even the children of the poorer classes to acquire a higher education. The same was true of the purchase of cars and modern household appliances.

A study by Professor Emile Sahliyeh titled *In Search of Leadership: West Bank Politics Since 1967*[17] indicates that the profound social changes occurring in the West Bank since 1967 have resulted in the modernization of its society. The employment structure changed, with large organizations such as professional unions, youth movements, and student groups being established. This development enabled the individual to interact with the community in a more direct manner, for in the traditional Arab society the individual's primary circle of association is his immediate family; the second circle is the extended family or clan *(hamulah)*; the third is his neighbors; and the last is a more extensive local group, be it religious or ethnic. The great importance ascribed to these bonds makes it difficult to break out of them and join more modern frameworks. Thus in the West Bank (as in much of the rest of the Arab world) it proved very difficult to create mass organizations, such as modern political parties, whose existence requires overcoming traditional ties and allegiances.

As to the search for leadership, it transpired that in the 1976 municipal elections in the West Bank, members of the wealthy and influential families were still being chosen for the municipal councils but the personalities elected tended to be the "black sheep" of these families. The mayor elected in Nablus was Bassam Shak'a, a maverick member of a prosperous local family. Unlike his brothers and uncles, he had never been a minister or member of Parliament in Jordan. Instead, Shak'a was a longtime activist in the Syrian *Ba'ath* Party, an advocate of militant Arab nationalism, and an opponent of the regime in Amman, which persecuted him for his activities and views. Men of a similar ilk were elected in Ramallah and al-Bireh.[18] In Hebron, Dr. Ahmed Hamze Natshe, a physician, had been a sure bet to win the mayoralty but he was deported by the military government on the eve of the vote. A member of the largest family in the Hebron area—a traditional family whose members generally mixed in conservative Muslim circles—Natshe was known as an activist in the Communist party. Like the other candidates in the 1976 municipal elections, he gathered around him a somewhat odd coalition of supporters. The public in Hebron backed him because of his radical social and political views, while his family tendered its support despite them.

Oddly enough, many of the leading PLO activists in the territories at the end of the 1980s also came from the ranks of the traditional elite. The sons of the Kanan family of Nablus, the Nusseibehs of Jerusalem, and the Qawasmehs of Hebron, whose fathers had been loyal servants of the Jordanian regime, threw their lot in with the PLO, as if they were the children of refugees from Haifa or Lydda. It is sometimes difficult to understand why children of the same Palestinian family decided to part ways, with some becoming officials in Amman and others embracing the Palestinian nationalism of the PLO. "When does a Palestinian living in Amman become a Jordanian?" a foreign journalist asked on a visit to the East Bank. "Whenever he decides to" was the reply.

In the West Bank decisions of that sort changed over the course of a few years. By the close of the 1950s, most members of the area's social elite had decided they were Jordanians. But the charged political and social climate of the 1980s prompted them to switch their allegiance and identify themselves as Palestinians.

In the summer of 1988, having lost his sway over the inhabitants of the territories, and grasping the implications of the *intifada*, King Hussein proclaimed the separation of the West Bank from the Kingdom of Jordan.[19] Fearing that the unrest in the territories would spill over the river and sweep the large Palestinian population on the East Bank, he assured his remaining Palestinian subjects that their rights would be honored like those of all Jordanian citizens.

The answer to the question Who is a Palestinian? is therefore more complex in the 1990s than ever before. The PLO holds meticulously to the old geographic definition, so that the Palestinian National Covenant still reads: "The Palestinians are Arabs who permanently resided in Palestine until 1947 . . . or anyone who was born to a Palestinian father after that date in Palestine or outside the country." In the 1990s, however, it would be more correct to say that a Palestinian is someone who identifies with the policy of that organization as the representative of his people. The geographical definition has largely been replaced by an ideological one.

The Palestinian national ideology, which in the past

had rested upon the central motif of return, added the element of "nation building": the fostering of tradition and striving for a sovereign state in the West Bank, East Jerusalem, and Gaza. Among the more prominent symbols of this ideology is the Palestinian national flag. A relatively new creation, it is essentially a copy of the flag that the Sherif Hussein of Mecca (King Hussein's great-grandfather) raised when, with the encouragement of the British, he led the Arab revolt against the dying Ottoman regime in June 1916. At that time the Arabs of Palestine flew an array of other flags—the banners of Nablus and Jerusalem, of Bedouin from Bet Shean and of Ibrahim al-Khalil from Hebron—that represented the traditionally "local" identities and were carried in parades and pilgrimage ceremonies.[20] Since the outbreak of the *intifada*, however, the Palestinians have used only the banner adopted by the PLO in 1964 and declared it the flag of Palestine. It has four colors— stripes of white, green, and black with a red triangle— evoking an old Arab nationalist poem: "White are our deeds, black is our battle, green are our fields, and red is our sword." The PLO has tried to hoist this old-new national flag above all the banners of the past as a symbol of the modern secular and democratic national values that will supersede the impotence of the old political and social orders. "O my defeated father, my humiliated mother, / To hell with the tribal tradition you have bequeathed me," wrote the poet Samih al-Qasim,[21] associating humiliation and defeat with the confining tradition of the past.

At the end of the 1980s, the struggle for the right to return was joined by a more emphatic aspect of the Palestinian identity: a popular uprising to drive out the occupiers and obtain some form of political independence. Exactly what kind of political independence do the Palestinians have in mind? A state in the West Bank and Gaza? A federation with Jordan (most of whose population is at any rate Palestinian)? A state in the territories as the initial stage toward establishing a single political entity in all of what once was Palestine?

The ultimate aim remains undefined. Yet the demand to return is unquestionably still part and parcel of all of the PLO's decisions and political statements. On November 15, 1988, at the close of the nineteenth session of the Palestine National Council, following the declaration of an independent state of Palestine, a statement was published lauding the *intifada* and demanding that Israel withdraw from the West Bank and Gaza. The call for self-determination and the establishment of a Palestinian state took precedence over manifesting the "right of return." Thus the sequence of events, as the PLO sees it, should now be: the convening of an international conference under UN auspices based on Security Council Resolutions 242 and 348; the dismantling of the Jewish settlements built in the territories after 1967; the constitution of a government in the territories under the protection of the UN during the interim period of negotiations on a political settlement; and only then "a solution to the problem of the Palestinian refugees in the spirit of the UN resolutions addressing the subject."[22] But there can be no doubt that in Palestinian eyes the solution must be to honor the rights of those who choose to return. Anyone who so desires is entitled to opt for a compromise and accept compensation for his home, property, and the suffering he has endured—"compensation for whoever does not wish to return to his homeland," as it was phrased in the resolutions of the Fez summit meeting. But in no Palestinian resolution or statement (including Arafat's declaration in Geneva just before the initiation of the dialogue with the United States) is there any concession whatsoever on the full right of return.

In the spring of 1988 the al-Hakawati Theater in East Jerusalem performed a play called *Kafr Shima* that deals with the yearning to return to a native village. In this play Kafr Shima is a small village whose houses were destroyed in 1948 and whose residents were scattered all over the globe. Some of them reached the Gulf states as refugees and prospered there, while others settled in the United States. All tried to forget their destroyed village. All but one man: Walid, the hero of the play, who studied in Cairo and then returned to see what had happened to Kafr Shima. Living among the ruins he finds Kawash, the village idiot, and the two set off on a long journey to refugee camps, the Arab countries, even the United States to track down the old inhabitants of the village and persuade them to return. "If we don't tell the tale of Kafr Shima," say the two protagonists at the end of the play, "it will fade, be forgotten, just as the village was razed."

Although the burden of exile continued to weigh heavily on the refugees from Kafr Shima, after forty years only the obsessed Walid and the village idiot tried to rekindle the yearning to return. Poised in the background of this play is the question: if a Palestinian state is established in the West Bank and the Gaza Strip, and even in East Jerusalem, what meaning will it have for the refugees of 1948? Will it provide a solution to the misery of the old residents of Kafr Shima and the two generations of their progeny—or for the residents of the Yarmuk camps on the outskirts of Damascus, or for those living around Tripoli and Beirut? Clearly, a sov-

ereign state in the West Bank and Gaza Strip is no solution for the exiles of 1948. The fact is that a good
proportion of the refugees who fled to Nablus then are
still living in Balata, Askar, and Ein Beit Alma—"temporary camps" on the outskirts of the city. What, then,
has a Palestinian state to offer the refugees of Ein Hilweh, near the Lebanese city of Sidon? The prospect of
"returning" to Nablus and crowding into Balata and
Askar? And if they are to live in a refugee camp, why
not stay in Ein Hilweh, where they feel comfortable,
rather than uproot themselves yet again merely to move
from one camp to another? Of course this predicament
applies not only to the refugees in the Arab countries
but also to those living in the occupied territories, especially the half-million inhabitants of the Gaza Strip.

No Palestinian scholar—or any other, for that matter
—has attempted a systematic study of just how many
families of 1948 refugees still demand the fulfillment of
their right to return. The Palestinians have raised a kind
of ideological barrier around this issue that does not
allow for any question about the desire of every last
refugee to return. Dr. Sharif Kana'ne of Bir-Zeit University confirms the impression, culled from conversations
with refugees, that those who continue to live in difficult conditions insist upon the right to return, rejecting
any substitute. Speaking to Israelis in the winter of
1989, for example, a young woman in the Shati refugee
camp on the Gaza coast said that the only solution acceptable to her and her friends was their resettlement
in the village of Hamama, north of Ashkelon. Asked
whether she wanted to drive off the people who had
been living there for over forty years, she replied eva-
sively: "There's room for everyone."

Not everyone is like-minded on this question, how-

ever. For refugee families who have rehabilitated themselves financially, and educated young people who
pursue a modern way of life, the demand to return has
become ideological in nature—more a matter of principle than the expression of a genuine desire. The owner
of a shoe store who lives comfortably in a suburb of
Bethlehem and whose children have received a higher
education concedes that he has lost all hope of returning to his native village of Zakariya. Yet he demands
suitable compensation for losing that village and, more
important, acknowledgment of his rights in the form of
an explicit admission that he and other members of the
village have been treated unjustly, not necessarily as
individuals but as a people. Recognition of his national
right to a state of his own would be considered "suitable compensation."

Back in the 1950s the poetess Fadwa Touqan wrote:
"I will return, and there will I close the book of my
life."[23] Touqan, it should be noted, is the daughter of a
wealthy and distinguished family from Nablus that had
never been cast out of its home. In making the pledge
"I will return," she was referring not to a concrete act
but rather to a desire for national "proprietorship."
Writing in a similar vein from the other side of the border, in Israel, Hanna Ibrahim from the village of Bina in
the Galilee called himself a refugee because he regarded
that designation as part of his national identity, even
though he had never left his home or his land.

And so it is with the overwhelming majority of the
1948 refugees: the longings for Sataf and Jaffa, Faluja
and Acre are collective rather than individual, longings
more for a national home rather than for a specific personal one that has since become the home of another.
Not that the refugees have waived their individual right

to return; after forty years, however, this right has acquired a broader and more abstract connotation as the prerogative of a collective with its own national tradition.

As long as the refugees insisted upon actually returning to their homes and lands, it was clear that there was no chance of negotiating a settlement with the State of Israel. The Palestinians boycotted Israel and denied its existence. Their demand to return to the actual site from which they had been displaced in 1948 clearly implied the destruction of the State of Israel. Only when the Palestinians had added another dimension to their thinking—the demands for rights in a national homeland—did the prospect of dialogue and negotiation with the State of Israel open.

This national return is no longer envisioned as a joyous victory parade but as a slow, sad convoy of "returnees and dreamers," as Mahmoud Darwish wrote in a long poem published in the summer of 1989.[24] Darwish describes the "returnees" of the late 1980s as people who, after "an absurd journey of exile," emerge "from the end of a long tunnel into the light . . . return from heroic stories to simple words, waving neither exultant hands nor flags to mark the miracle." They return weary from the sea and desert air, without specifying the borders, homes, and villages to which they are headed. "They return," Darwish writes in the plural about his people, "but I shall not return"—as though he were reconciled to the fact that even if the Palestinian national solution comes to fruition, it will not necessarily include his own return to the village of Birwa in the Galilee, for Birwa is no more.

ACKNOWLEDGMENTS

The most comprehensive research on Palestinian refugees was done by a group of scholars at Bir-Zeit University headed by Dr. Sharif Kana'ne, who placed at my disposal monographs and maps he has published and the data he has accumulated over the years and whose meetings with me were most helpful. I have also quoted extensively from works of Palestinian literature and drawn upon the writings of Shimon Ballas; the journal *Mifgash*, edited by Muhammad Hamzeh Ghnaim; the studies of Mahmoud Abbasi, including his work on the development of the novel and short story in Israeli-Arab literature; and the articles and essays of George Kanaze, Jamil Shalhout, and others.

The first analysis of the "vision of return" was done by Professor Abdul-Latif Tibawi of Harvard University at the beginning of the 1960s, and it has maintained its great value to this day. I have drawn heavily on data and estimates given in the most thorough research on the creation of the refugee problem in 1948, Benny Morris's work *The Birth of the Palestinian Refugee Problem, 1947–1949*, as well as on the anthology *Arav ve-Yisrael* [The Arabs and Israel] (Tel Aviv: Am Oved and the Truman Institute, 1975); issues of *Hamizrach Hehadash* [The New East], which contain a wide variety of articles, surveys, and translations of documents; the publications of the Van Leer Institute in Jerusalem; the books and research of Dr. Meron Benvenisti, who directed the West Bank and Gaza Project; and the lexicon edited by Ya'akov Shimoni.

As to the Arabic names, I have occasionally departed from the usual system of transliteration in the interests of easing things for the reader.

I owe a special debt of gratitude to Dr. Shalom Goldman of Dartmouth College, who went over the manuscript, made corrections, and invested much thought and attention as an editor. His familiarity with the subject and his command of Hebrew and Arabic made his contribution of very special value. I also wish to thank Mr. Moshe Shalvi for his help and care in drafting parts of the translation and to Jennifer Ash of Random House for her dedication and diligence in carrying the book through publication.

Danny Rubinstein
Jerusalem, July 1991

NOTES

1. VICTIMS OF THE MAP

1. The circumstances in which the refugees were up-rooted are described at length in Benny Morris, *The Birth of the Palestinian Refugee Problem, 1947–1949* (Cambridge: Cambridge University Press, 1967).

2. Report of the general commissioner of UNRWA on the Palestinian refugees in the Near East submitted to the General Assembly in 1988.

3. UNRWA defines a Palestinian refugee as a man who usually lives in Palestine and lost his home and sources of livelihood as a result of hostilities and who is in need of aid. Those entitled to welfare are determined according to this definition. UNRWA added two important elements to the definition: (1) that welfare would be accorded to those who lived in the country permanently at least two years prior to 1948; and (2) welfare would be accorded to a refugee and all of his offspring until their return to their homes, in line with the UN resolutions.

4. "The Identity of Absence," *Mifgash* [Encounter] 7–8 (1987): 46. Darwish ascribes the term "exiles from history and homeland" to the Jews as well.

5. The title of his collection of Palestinian poems, *Victims of the Map* (London: Saai Books, 1984).

6. Edward Said, *The Question of Palestine* (New York: Vintage Books, 1980), p. 124.

7. Morris, *Palestinian Refugee Problem*, chapter 5.

8. "In the Crater of a Volcano," *Mifgash* [Encounter] 7–8 (1987): 72.

2. THE HOUSE OVER THE BORDER

1. A list of 369 villages that were destroyed appears in the preface to Morris. See also Kamel Abdel Fatah, ed., *The Map of the Destroyed Villages, 1948–1950* [in Arabic] (Bir-Zeit: Bir-Zeit University).

2. *Sataf as an Example of the Reconstruction of Mountain Agriculture* [in Hebrew] (Jewish National Fund, 1988).

3. Sefi Ben-Yosef, ed., *Guide to Israel*, vol. 10 [in Hebrew] (Jerusalem: Keter, Ministry of Defense Publishing House, n.d.), p. 98.

4. Meron Benvenisti, *Hakela ve-ha-Alah* [Conflicts and Contradictions] (Jerusalem: Keter, 1988), p. 132.

5. *The Holocaust, the Destruction of Jerusalem, and the Lost Paradise, 1947–1955.* It may not be a coincidence that in the title of his book Aref al-Aref uses the traditional Muslim name for Jerusalem, Beit al-Quds ("the Holy House"). This name was given to the city during the early days of Islam and was taken from the term "the Temple," which is what the Jews called the city at the time.

6. Said, *Question of Palestine*, p. 182.

7. As happened, for example, in the Musrara neighborhood at the end of the Street of the Prophets in Jerusalem, when a number of the Arab residents moved to the eastern side of the street.

8. Morris, *Palestinian Refugee Problem*, pp. 237 ff.

9. Fawaz Turki, *The Disinherited: Journal of a Palestinian Exile* (New York: Monthly Review Press, 1972), p. 8.

10. The name of a well-known novel by Issa Neouri (Beirut: Awidat Press, 1954).

11. The name of a play by Abdel-Rahman al-Sharqawi published in *Dar al-Sharq* (1970).

12. Emil Habibi, *The "Opsimist": The Wondrous Chronicle of the Disappearance of Said Abu al Nakhs al-Mitshaal*, trans. Anton Shammas [in Hebrew] (Jerusalem: Mifras, 1984), p. 34.

13. See Shimon Ballas, *Arabic Literature in the Shadow of War* [in Hebrew] (Tel Aviv: Am Oved, 1978), p. 44. Arguments of this sort are often raised in Zurayek's books *The Meaning of the Catastrophe* [in Arabic] (Beirut: Dar al-Alam Lilmalayn, 1948) and *The Reinterpretation of the Catastrophe* [in Arabic] (Beirut: Dar al-Alam Lilmalayn, 1967). An overview of these books can be found in Yehoshafat Harkabi *The Arab Position in the Israeli-Arab Conflict* [in Hebrew] (Tel Aviv: Dvir, 1968).

14. *That's How I Am, Gentlemen: Excerpts from the Diary of Khalil Sakakini*, trans. Gideon Shiloh [in Hebrew] (Jerusalem: Keter, 1990).

15. "The Flight from Tulkarem" in *Palestinian Stories*, ed. Shimon Ballas [in Hebrew] (Tel Aviv: Eked, 1970).

16. "Land of the Sad Oranges," *ibid.*

17. Morris, *Palestinian Refugee Problem*, p. 144.

18. *Ibid.*, p. 127.

19. *Ibid.*, p. 136.

20. *Ibid.*, p. 228.

21. For complete details on the conduct of the leaders of the Arab community during these years, see Yehosuha Porat, *From Riots to a State: The Arab National Movement 1929–1939* [in Hebrew] (Tel Aviv: Am Oved, 1978).

22. Especially in Habibi, *The "Opsimist,"* chapters 5–8.

23. The Reconciliation Conference in Lausanne was convened on the initiative of the UN General Assembly in December 1948. Eliyahu Sasson's reports appear in *Documents on the Foreign Policy of the State of Israel*, vol. 4, May–December 1949 [in Hebrew] (Jerusalem: State Archives, 1986). See, for example, p. 93.

3. THE LOST PARADISE

1. Turki, *Disinherited*, p. 72.

2. Mahmoud Abbasi, "Uncle Hassan's Return to His Homeland," *Mifgash* [Encounter] 10–11 (1988): 129.

3. *Ibid.*

4. Documentary film by Ayal Sivan.

5. David Grossman, *Koteret Rashit* [Headlines] (April 29, 1987), p. 12.

6. Sivan's film.

7. Faisal al-Hourani, spring 1989.

8. Raja Shehadeh, *Ha-derekh Ha-shlishit* [The Third Way] (Jerusalem: Adam Publishers, 1982), p. 92.

9. Article on Jabra's poetry by Salman Masalkhah in *Ha'aretz*, March 24, 1989.

4. THE OBLIGATION TO REMEMBER

1. Bir-Zeit University: Center for Documentation and Research, series on destroyed Arab villages [in Arabic].

2. Adnan Abdul-Razzeq, "Changes in the Family Life of the Arab Refugees in Refugee Camps" (master's thesis, Hebrew University, Jerusalem, 1977).

3. *Without a Homeland: Conversations with Eric Rouleau* [in Hebrew] (Jerusalem: Mifras, 1979), pp. 23 ff.

4. Conversation with Sharif Kana'ne, spring 1989.

5. *Ibid.*

6. Turki, *Disinherited*, p. 16.

7. Conversation with refugees in Ein Hilweh, summer 1982. See also A.-L. Tibawi, "Visions of the Return," *Middle East Journal* (1963): 510.

8. Sivan's film.

9. As related to author in the camp in the summer of 1985.

10. As related to author in Gaza in the winter of 1988.

5. THE EXPERIENCE OF LOSS

1. See Morris, *Palestinian Refugee Problem,* pp. 48 ff.

2. Eliyahu Sasson; and see Morris, *ibid.,* p. 83.

3. See Morris, *ibid.,* pp. 94–95.

4. S. Yizhar, *"Khirbet Hizah"* in *Four Stories* [in Hebrew] (Tel Aviv: Hakibbutz Hameuchad, 1967), pp. 59–71.

5. See Ballas, *Arabic Literature,* p. 58. The story takes place in June 1967, and the father-in-law is a refugee from 1948.

6. *Politika* 4 (1985): 11.

7. See *Shdemot* (periodical), Summer 1977 (*Mapam* Archive).

8. Moshe Dayan, *Living with the Bible* (Jerusalem: Edanim; London: Weidenfeld and Nicolson, 1978), p. 144.

9. Ezra Danin's work regarding the refugees is discussed in Ya'akov Sharett, *Ezra Danin: A Zionist for All Seasons* [in Hebrew] (Jerusalem: Kidum, 1987).

10. *Ibid.,* vol. II, p. 669.

11. Tibawi, "Visions of the Return," p. 510.

12. *Mifgash* [Encounter] 7–8 (1987): 46.

13. Benvenisti, *Hakela ve-ha-Alah,* pp. 143–144.

14. Conversation with author.

6. A TICKET HOME

1. See Turki, *Disinherited,* p. 67.

2. See Tibawi, "Visions of the Return," p. 513

3. *Ibid.,* pp. 511–514.

4. *Ibid.,* p. 523.

5. *Ibid.,* p. 515.

6. *Ibid.*, p. 524.

7. Yehoshafat Harkabi, ed., *The Arabs and Israel: Decisions of the Palestinian National Council* [in Hebrew] (Tel Aviv–Jerusalem: Am Oved, The Truman Institute, 1975), p. 30.

8. *Ibid.*, p. 39.

9. *Ibid.*, p. 65.

10. Said, *Question of Palestine*, p. 74.

7. A VOYAGE OF DELUSION

1. See Habibi, *The "Opsimist,"* p. 129.

2. For a description of the expulsion from Lydda and Ramle, see Morris, *Palestinian Refuge Problem*, pp. 204 ff.

3. A detailed critique of the story is in Ballas, *Arabic Literature*, pp. 72 ff.

4. Ehud Ya'ari, *Strike Terror: The Story of Fatah* (Tel Aviv: Lewin-Epstein, 1970), pp. 82 ff.

8. REFUGEES IN THEIR HOME

1. See Morris, *Palestinian Refugee Problem*, map 2.

2. Primarily the Absentee Property Law of 1950 based on emergency regulations from the end of 1948.

3. George Kanaze, "The Question of Identity in Israeli-Arab Literature," *One Out of Every Six Israelis*, ed. Alouph Hareven [in Hebrew] (Jerusalem: Van Leer Institute, 1981), p. 156.

4. See the description of the affair by one of the participants, Sabri Jereis, *The Arabs in Israel* [in Hebrew] (Haifa, 1966), p. 117.

5. Translation from Arabic into Hebrew by Avraham Yinon, *The New East* 15 (1965): 57–58.

6. Ballas, *Arabic Literature*, p. 74.

7. Ibid., p. 84.

8. Taken from the poem "Ten Impossible Things," *Mifgash* [Encounter] 9 (1988): 79.

9. See Ballas, *Arabic Literature*, p. 84.

10. Quoted in Ian Lustick, *Arabs in the Jewish State* [in Hebrew] (Haifa: Mifras, 1985), pp. 26–27.

9. ARE YOU SUBLETTING?

1. Anton Shammas, "At Half Mast," *Politika* 28 (1989): 23.

2. Ballas, *Arabic Literature,* pp. 67–69.

3. Contact was made immediately between the veteran activists of the Israeli Communist party and its counterpart in Jordan. Both were members of the same political organization: the League for National Liberation.

4. See Ballas, *Arabic Literature,* p. 70.

5. The Palestinian National Front was active in the territories at the beginning of the 1970s with the aid and backing of the Communists.

6. The National Guidance Committee was founded after the signing of the Camp David agreement in 1978 to galvanize the public in the territories against it.

7. Conversation with author on the results of the 1988 elections to the Knesset.

8. The PLO repeated this statement a number of times, and Faisal al-Husseini reiterated it at a news conference in East Jerusalem on September 28, 1989.

9. *Ha-Aravim Ezrakhei Yisrael* [Israel's Arab citizens] (Jerusalem: Ministry of Education and Culture, Van Leer Institute, 1988), p. 151.

10. *Ibid.*

11. *Ibid.,* p. 150.

12. The more prominent studies in this sphere were done by the Jewish-Arab Center at the University of Haifa.

13. Shammas, "At Half Mast," p. 22.

14. See *Israel's Arab Citizens,* p. 104.

15. *Ibid.*

16. See, e.g., Gideon Beiger, *Moshevet Keter o Bayit*

Leumi [A crown colony or national home] (Jerusalem: Ben-Zvi Institute, 1983), chapter 1.

17. See *Gesher* (A Palestinian weekly in Hebrew), November 18, 1988.

18. Shammas, "At Half Mast," p. 25.

10. THE UNITY OF THE TWO RIVERBANKS

1. Muhammad Abu-Shilbaya, *O Jerusalem* [in Arabic] (Jerusalem: al-Quds Publishing House, 1974).

2. See Daniel Rubinstein, "The Jerusalem Municipality under the Ottomans, British and Jordanians" in *Jerusalem, Problems and Prospects,* ed. Joel L. Kramer (New York: Praeger, 1980), pp. 72 ff.

3. See Asher Susser, *Between Jordan and Palestine* [in Hebrew] (Tel Aviv: Hakibbutz Hameuchad, 1983), chapters 3–4.

11. STATE LANDS

1. Said in the presence of journalists in the summer of 1969.

2. At a conference in the Hebron Municipality in the autumn of 1975.

3. The paper began to appear in the summer of 1972 together with *al-Fajr.* Both represent the positions of the PLO.

4. For a detailed analysis of this phenomenon see Gideon Shiloh, *Israeli Arabs in the Eyes of the Arab States and the PLO* [in Hebrew] (Jerusalem: Magnes, 1982).

5. The translation from Arab to Hebrew is by Shiloh, *ibid.,* p. 52, Ballas, *Arabic Literature,* p. 82, and my own free translation.

6. Shiloh, *Israeli Arabs,* p. 53.

7. For demographic statistics on the territories see Meron Benvenisti, *The West Bank Handbook* (Jerusalem: Jerusalem Post, 1986), pp. 51–54.

8. *Ibid.,* p. 89.

9. Col. David Farhi in 1973.

10. As related to the author in his home in 1969. A while later Qamhawi was deported from Nablus and appointed to the PLO Executive.

11. See Benvenisti, *The West Bank Handbook*, pp. 113–121.

12. *Ibid.*, p. 30.

13. The writer and journalist David Shaham, head of the International Center for Peace.

14. *Gesher*, October 7, 1988.

15. See Benvenisti, *The West Bank Handbook*, pp. 223–225.

16. Akram Haniyeh, "That Village . . . That Morning" in *Beyond the Near Horizon* [in Hebrew] (Jerusalem: Keter, 1989), p. 111.

17. *Gesher*, October 7, 1988.

12. BUT I SHALL NOT RETURN

1. See Dov Shenar, "The Media and Nation-Building in the West Bank," *Mifgash* [Encounter] 7–8 (1987): 52.

2. The term used by Emanuel Sivan in his book *Arab Political Myths* [in Hebrew] (Tel Aviv: Am Oved, 1988), pp. 202–209.

3. *Gesher*, September 22, 1987.

4. Among the works published was an album of drawings of Palestinian costumes by the artists Suleiman Mansur and Nabil Anani. Exhibitions of the Association for the Family were held in al-Bireh and in the Museum of the Center for the Palestinian-Arab Popular Heritage in East Jerusalem.

5. Eighteen studies in these fields were published in the journal *Heritage and Society* [in Arabic].

6. For example, in the Deheishe refugee camp and in the towns of al-Bireh and Beit Sahur. These troupes work in collaboration with the colleges and student councils in the territories.

7. By Ali al-Khalili, Nablus.

8. Four studies in these fields, relating to the Ramallah district, were published by Dr. Barghouti, and one study, on the Hebron district, was published by Dr. Rushdi al-Ashab.

9. By Ali al-Khalili, Nablus.

10. By Ra'id Abu Hashish.

11. By Zaki al-Ila.

12. By Jamil Shalhut, Dr. Mohammed Shehadeh, and Ali Otman.

13. Some of these studies were published by the Arab Center for Culture and the Arts founded in al-Hakawati in East Jerusalem.

14. Primarily in the Arab colleges and the Institute for Arab Studies in East Jerusalem headed by Faisal al-Husseini.

15. Sivan, *Arab Political Myths*, p. 141.

16. See *Judea, Samaria, and the Gaza District, 1967–1987* (Jerusalem: Carta-Ministry of Defense, 1987).

17. Emile Sahliyeh, *In Search of Leadership: West Bank Politics Since 1967* (Washington: Brookings Institution, 1988).

18. Karim Khalaf in Ramallah and Ibrahim al-Tawil in al-Bireh.

19. The Jordanian government had published an ambitious five-year plan in 1986 that was to have sent $1.25 billion flowing into the West Bank and Gaza for development. The plan was never carried out.

20. See Dr. Mahdi Abdul Hadi, *The Development of the Arab Flag* [in Arabic] (Jerusalem, 1986).

21. See Kanaze, "The Question of Identity," p. 152.

22. This wording of the political announcement was published in *Gesher*, November 18, 1988.

23. See Tibawi, "Visions of the Return," p. 517.

24. The poem, "The Tragedy of Narcissus and the Silver Joke," was published in June 1989 in *al-Yom a-*

Sabe, an Arabic journal printed in Paris. In translating and interpreting the poem I was aided by Semadar Perry of the Hebrew daily *Yediot Aharonot* and the poet Salman Masalkhah.

ABOUT THE AUTHOR

DANNY RUBINSTEIN, an Israeli journalist for more than twenty years, is one of the most respected observers of the Palestinian scene. In 1988, he received the Sokolow Prize, Israel's equivalent of the Pulitzer. He writes for the daily *Ha'aretz* and lives in Jerusalem.